Remembering

KANNAPOLIS

Remembering KANNAPOLIS

Tales from Towel City

Helen Arthur-Cornett

Charleston · London

The History PRESS

Published by The History Press
Charleston, SC   29403
www.historypress.net

Cover image: 1968 postcard of Cannon Mills.

First published 2006

Manufactured in the United Kingdom

ISBN-10 1.59629.073.0
ISBN-13 978.1.59629.073.0

Library of Congress Cataloging-in-Publication Data

Arthur-Cornett, Helen.
  Remembering Kannapolis : tales from Towel City / Helen Arthur-Cornett.
    p. cm.
  ISBN-13: 978-1-59629-073-0 (alk. paper)
  ISBN-10: 1-59629-073-0 (alk. paper)
  1. Kannapolis (N.C.)--History--Anecdotes. 2. Kannapolis (N.C.)--Social
life and customs--Anecdotes. 3. Kannapolis (N.C.)--Biography--Anecdotes.
I. Title.
  F264.K35A78 2006
  975.6'72--dc22
  2006031695

Notice: The information in this book is true and complete to the best of our knowledge. It is offered without guarantee on the part of the author or The History Press. The author and The History Press disclaim all liability in connection with the use of this book.

Contents

Contents

Contents

Preface

$\mathcal{I}$t seems ironic that this book, *Remembering Kannapolis*, is being published as Kannapolis celebrates its hundredth year—and as much of the hundred-year-old familiar face of the downtown has disappeared with the demolition of those sturdy old Cannon Mills plants.

Of course it is for good cause. Billionaire David Murdock's monumental plan to transform this vintage mill town into a futuristic nutrition and diet research center—joined by the University of North Carolina, North Carolina State University and Duke University—will forever change the face of old Kannapolis.

The project is expected to attract thousands of high tech researchers, provide thousands of new jobs for local people and bring in thousands of new workers' families, plus businesses, industries, professional and service agencies.

So Kannapolis will never be the same. Even the big lake in mid-downtown was drained and a huge brick food research center is going up in its bed. The YMCA, with its thousands of members and its myriad activities, is gone. Cannon Mills, Fieldcrest Cannon, the other companies which for so long made Kannapolis an exceptional mill town, too, are now gone forever.

Preface

So it is with both sadness and joy that we begin the publishing process to produce an anecdotal history of old Kannapolis, through many columns I've written for the *Charlotte Observer*'s "A Look Back" column and some special old photographs.

Through these columns and photographs of our Towel City, we'll tell the story of significant or interesting Kannapolis people and their doings. It won't be a complete history, of course, as my local history columns are mainly designed to entertain as well as to inform. They are, of course, as accurate as I and the demanding editors at the *Charlotte Observer* can make them.

I've never believed in "out with the old, in with the new" because what is old is still dear to many of us.

Kannapolis was once the biggest unincorporated town in the Southeast, they've told us. What tomorrow may bring is still unknown, but we can show through *Remembering Kannapolis* what Kannapolis was, beginning in 1906.

Can we try to make efforts toward further preservation of things Kannapolis? Its cotton mill heritage should not disappear, as did those massive Cannon plants.

Acknowledgements

To the *Charlotte Observer* and *Cabarrus Neighbors* and their editors and staffs go my deep appreciation for their help and support in publishing this book—again taken from my "Look Back" columns of local history. From the start, they have generously given me all necessary permissions and photographs. Without their cooperation, this or the first two books compiled from columns would not have been possible.

Again, my special thanks must go to Scott Verner, editor of the *Observer*'s *Cabarrus Neighbors*, who contributed so much in more ways than I can name.

So thank you, thank you all. My deepest appreciation.

Special thanks also must go to Larry Hayer and the History Room of the Kannapolis branch, Cabarrus County Library System. Without Larry's help and his expertise in several fields—especially computers—my hands would have been tied.

To you readers of "Look Back," who have so generously contributed those precious bits and pieces of our history, I can only thank you also from the bottom of my heart. Your contributions have broadened and expanded the base of historic items that we have collected over the years. They have all been compelling or amusing or tragic or wonderful glimpses of past ways of life. And I thank you.

Several names come to mind—Bill Workman for his 1920s memories of Kannapolis, historian J.K. Rouse, Mary Lore Flowe for her information on Israel Pickens, Triece family descendants, Hank Utley for his baseball series, retired editor Tom Wingate, Dr. Gary Freeze for his contributions on the Cannon families, the descendants of John Baker who worked hard on his cemetery, Judge Clarence Horton, Jim Johnson, W.E. Bostian for his lovable mule story—and of course our fun-loving anonymous letter writer.

I feel sure I'm missing some who should be named—but please forgive. All of you are important in preserving these appealing bits of our history.

Thanks to you, you've made my work easy—so easy that I still enjoy and still love writing the history of Cabarrus County through these columns.

1.

Glass: A Village Before Kannapolis Was Born

Sunday, December 15, 1991

In 1886 Cabarrus County resident John Peter Triece and his bride, Maggie Louela Earnhardt Triece, settled down to their life together in Glass, North Carolina.

Glass?

In the 1880s it was a small community in north Cabarrus County, where John Peter Triece built the first general store. Today, though it has almost disappeared, the few remains of little Glass lie in a heavily populated, heavily developed and heavily traveled South Kannapolis.

In 1886 the area that was to become Kannapolis and home of internationally known Cannon Mills was "only hundreds of acres of woods, broom sage and cotton fields," writes Dot Massey, Kannapolis native and a granddaughter of Maggie and John Peter Triece. Kannapolis itself was still just a gleam in the eye of future textile magnate James W. Cannon. For many years, the Glass sign stood beside the railroad, near a platform that held a

Triece Store, the first business in the Kannapolis area, was opened by John Peter Triece in the village of Glass, which eventually disappeared into a growing Kannapolis. Peter's wife, Maggie, is seated in front of the store. The old building survives today as the Book Trader.

big hook for trains to pick up or deliver bags of mail. The sign is now gone, and only local old-timers recall the sleepy hamlet.

While Kannapolis has absorbed the 1880s Glass community, Massey's lively account has preserved a bit of its history. John Peter Triece prospered, she writes, and his Triece General Store long was a gathering place. One customer was J.W. Cannon, who founded Cannon Mills Company. He "often stopped by Triece General Store to buy fresh eggs, butter and chickens from Mrs. Triece.

"James Cannon and John Peter were good friends and often went hunting together.

"Charlie [Charles A.] Cannon, who later took over his father's growing textile industry, was a regular customer at Triece's."

Glass was named after Fred Glass, a major landowner and the postmaster, who collected outgoing mail to load it on trains from the platform and sorted incoming mail for delivery by Glass's

An unidentified motorcyclist, possibly stationmaster John Thomas McBride Rogers, on his vintage bike in a photo of the Glass Depot. Trains didn't stop, so incoming mail was tossed on the platform and trainmen grabbed the outgoing mail off hooks. The depot disappeared in the 1950s.

one postman, Fernie Rogers, who then delivered it by horse and buggy. "In the winter [Rogers] would heat bricks and put them in the buggy to keep his feet warm," Massey wrote. "It would take him all day long to finish his route." The Glass post office was located on the village's main intersection.

Later, with growing success, John Peter Triece expanded his operation, adding a cotton gin, a blacksmith shop, a sawmill and a planer house, where sawed wood was taken to be finished, Massey wrote.

Numbers of Cabarrus and Rowan farmers and business people gathered there to have their cotton ginned, their horses and mules shod and their logs turned into lumber. While waiting, they could exchange news, gossip or shop in the general store.

In fact, in 1887 "some of the first lumber was sawed and sold to James Cannon to begin construction of Cannon Mills textile

The little Glass community, before Kannapolis absorbed it, had various activities for its families. Village-wide picnics were among the favorite down home doings.

company, and for mill houses," Massey wrote. "In 1913, John Peter added a woodwork shop on the side of the general store" where he built furniture, tables, chairs, swings and the like. "He built the first benches for Center Grove Lutheran Church."

The Trieces had eight children, a big help as the family's various businesses grew. After John Peter's death, the youngest child, Bill Triece, ran the company.

Later Bill Triece added the Independent Coal Company, which eventually converted to selling oil—the first fuel oil business in Kannapolis.

In 1903 Glass got into mainstream of the modern world, Massey wrote, with construction of the first Concord Telephone exchange in Triece's General Store.

But "it was moved in 1908 to Kannapolis in a room upstairs over F.L. Smith Drug Store that was on the square in Kannapolis.

"There were fifty pairs of cables that could serve seven hundred to eight hundred phone subscribers. There were from eight to twenty-two people on a party line." Can you imagine today's teens with a party line of eight to twenty-two people?

Alas, most of the Triece buildings were torn down eventually, and Citizens National Bank was built on that site. Fortunately, the Triece General Store building still stands—although it was moved across the street. Can you believe Kannapolis's historic old store is still useful today as a sportswear shop?

2.

Historian Tells How Jim Cannon Built Kannapolis

Sunday, May 8, 1992

Why is there a Kannapolis anyway? asked historian Dr. Gary Freeze, provoking a kind of bemused silence among Kannapolis History Associates Monday night. But then came, "Concord in the 1890s was a nasty place…violent, populist."

The 1992 annual meeting of the increasingly active Kannapolis History Associates proved an evening double rich in history with the good professor's commentaries. The society first presented two plaques to venerable Kannapolis historian J.K. Rouse for his ten well-researched books on local history.

Then came Gary Freeze's intriguing account of young Jim Cannon, whose successful 1880s venture into the world of textiles changed the course of county history and eventually led to the building of Kannapolis. Freeze, a lively Erskine College professor, discussed "Young Jim Cannon and the New South" with his usual compelling blend of impish humor and hard facts. He described in colorful fashion how the new Kannapolis was born, seven miles

James W. Cannon was the mastermind, the builder of Kannapolis, where his Cannon Mills soared to cotton mill fame over many years. His son, Charles A. Cannon, took up where Mr. J.W. left off and guided the company to international renown with its sheets and towels.

While Mr. Jim's textile empire was centered in Kannapolis, his substantial home was located on tree-lined North Union Street in Concord, seven miles to the south.

This office is where "Mr. Jim" worked every day, building his Cannon Mills, overseeing every aspect of the mills he built as well as his textile town, Kannapolis, also built to his specifications.

north of old Concord, due to the Cannon father-son duo—J.W. and Charles Cannon Sr.—who guided Cannon Mills sheets and towels to international recognition.

Freeze, a lively, knowledgeable speaker, declared that Cannon wasn't exactly a rags-to-riches Horatio Alger story. His folks were solid farming people, back in the years before and after the Civil War. But young Jim Cannon did start from scratch and became a roaring success—a genuine textile baron of his era.

However, the full Cannon story is yet to be told, Freeze told the Kannapolis History Associates. And he should know. In 1978, as he began researching the Odell story—rummaging through Library of Congress records, old documents in Boston, even Odell family closets in Atlanta—the Cannon story emerged at every point.

Now, folks, historian Freeze knows Cabarrus textiles inside out. He researched and wrote his doctoral dissertation on the old Odell (which later bore the names Locke and Randolph) Mill and the Odell family—and along the way absorbed the Cannon Mills story as well.

Monday night's crowd of eighty-plus was all ears as he told it. "I don't know for sure why there's a Kannapolis," Gary Freeze began, "but I have some guesses." They begin with the fact that Captain Odell's 1880s Odell Manufacturing had transformed Concord from a quiet crossroads village to a burgeoning, booming New South town. Concord even had suburbs, such as Forest Hill. It also meant that around Concord "land was becoming pricey," Freeze continued.

But back in the 1890s, prosaic Concord may not have been ready for young Jim Cannon's progressive ideas. Town fathers had voted down a proposal to install sewer facilities. Efforts to get city streets paved failed, despite influence exerted by the Cannons as well as the Odells, who had pulled Concord and Cabarrus County through the depression of 1893, the historian allowed. "Jim Cannon also understood that electricity was going to be the way of the future," even though the Odells were still using wood and steam in their mill operations—and this meant they were also cutting down all the trees.

Then young Jim Cannon ran for the Concord City Council. He lost. "I don't think he ever ran for office again," Freeze said.

Jim Cannon was a silent man who was driven to success. Whatever his reaction might have been, instead of building his Cannon Mill in the Concord area, Jim Cannon bought acreage in a sedge field several miles to the north to launch his Kannapolis. "He probably realized he'd be better off by himself," Freeze theorized, where he could start out right and build his town to his standards.

Freeze's colorful comments were much too much to cover in one article. And he didn't elaborate on that intriguing comment about violence in Concord. But he elaborated on young Jim Cannon of the New South.

James William Cannon was born near Mecklenburg County's historic Sugaw Creek Presbyterian Church on April 25, 1852. At fourteen, he began his illustrious career as an errand boy and clerk in a Charlotte grocery store.

Jim Cannon's early life was one of stern religious upbringing and work ethic instilled by his parents. They even had an altar in their home. The Cannons were Presbyterians who instilled in their children the values of faith, family, sharing, self-reliance and respect for others and their ideas.

"Jim Cannon was a product of that community," Freeze said. "There was nothing to suggest he was born with a silver spoon in his mouth. He came out of a great farming middle class. Jim Cannon never forgot that. He never put on airs. He'd set out in a simple wagon, visit farmers and their families." In fact, he traveled "barefoot some of the time," Gary Freeze reported. Jim Cannon also was fortunate to have been born in the fertile "blackjack" belt that gave Cabarrus County farmers "wondrous success growing cotton."

By nineteen, Cannon was a partner with his brother David in a Concord general store, having bought out original partner James Long's interest. Soon, young Jim branched out into cotton buying, which brought him success in ever-widening circles—and later it brought him valuable business contacts in the North.

With his blonde hair and chestnut brown eyes "that fairly danced in their sockets," and by sheer hard work and force of personality, Jim Cannon early on had worked up to becoming the most popular cotton buyer in Concord, Freeze said. Furthermore, he paid top prices. But more importantly, young Jim had "the talents the Creator gave him" to create, then drive his textile undertaking to success. Remember, this was in a time when the South was "cash-poor and cotton-rich," Freeze said. One year, neighboring Mecklenburg farmers formed a parade of cotton-loaded wagons out of Charlotte bearing signs stating, "This cotton is going to Concord."

"Cotton was half-a-cent higher in Concord. That was a lot then."

Oddly, Jim Cannon's high cotton prices benefited everybody, Freeze said. "Odell Mills was sucking up every fiber of cotton in three counties. The farmers made more money, and the Odells made money."

Eventually, Mary Ella Bost became Jim Cannon's bride. She proved a boon to young Cannon, for in 1887, along with his other associates, she helped him raise the money to build his mill. By 1888, Jim Cannon's first four-thousand-spindle mill was in operation. His Cabarrus Cotton Mill was built in 1892. Then came plants in China Grove, Albemarle, Salisbury and Mount Pleasant, which were making "a useful, durable weave called Cannon Cloth."

In 1907 he started Kannapolis as a "model mill town" called "Towel City." He planned it to have good, affordable homes, paved roads, churches, stores and social and recreational facilities—and that it did. Jim Cannon even financed Kannapolis's first school.

An interesting sidelight, revealed by Gary Freeze: in the late 1800s, Dunn and Bradstreet described Jim Cannon as sober and genteel, a man who had succeeded without important connections.

"There was a sense of vigor, of drive about Jim Cannon," Freeze said. "A feeling that he was going to go places—and take others with him."

A popular folk tale about Jim Cannon appeared in *Fortune* magazine in the 1930s: it was his habit to get in a simple wagon, to ride the county and visit individual farmers in person. "He was willing to get as dusty as everyone else," Gary Freeze said. He also kept a very personal relationship with his workers. In hard times, "he would tell them, 'Our wages may be cut,' not [his workers'] wages," the historian said.

During one depression, Jim Cannon bought up all the bankrupt farmers' cotton and stored it in his warehouses, and when prices went up, he sold it back to them—at the price he had bought it—to let the farmers sell it at the higher price. By helping the community in such ways, Jim Cannon also helped himself, Gary Freeze said.

His son, Charles, who later propelled Cannon Mills Company's sheets and towels into international recognition, continued those community-conscious principles.

"Jim Cannon had a sense of marketing that the Odells never had," Freeze explained. "He opened an office in New York. He took a page from the Dukes by using his name as a brand name. He was astute in new technologies" of that era, and while the Odells continued manufacturing linen towels, Jim Cannon knew terry cloth was the wave of the future.

Jim Cannon also was lucky, Freeze said, listing several "ifs" that could have blocked Cannon's drive to success: If he hadn't been born to a high-principled, deeply religious family with strong work ethic and high standards; if he hadn't been born in a community with deep textile roots; if Concord hadn't already become a great cotton mill town, dating from the 1830s; if the Odells hadn't paved the way with their successful textile mills—without all those "ifs," Freeze theorized, Jim Cannon might not have changed the course of Cabarrus economic history.

"Why he succeeded in wonderful, even mysterious ways is a story yet to be told. My suspicion is that he was a man driven to success."

Freeze ended his remarks on a provocative note—namely, as to how Kannapolis got its name. Many have claimed it came from the Greek word kanna, for looms, to become "City of Looms," Freeze explained.

"Well, that just isn't so," he said, allowing as how he'd discovered some early references to Kannapolis that instead contained the name "Cannonville."

But then, I don't remember that Gary Freeze told the history associates exactly how Kannapolis did get its name.

Jim Cannon's Monumental Impact Lives On

Sunday, April 12, 1992

They called him Jim, that young Cannon fellow who had a dream and a lot of ambition, back in 1888. He was energetic, too. Today, modern folks might term him a go-getter, a self-starter, a mover and shaker. Seems he was all of that.

All Jim Cannon's basic, homespun attributes seem to have led to the giant textile empire that became, and remained for many years, a bulwark of Cabarrus County's economy—Cannon Mills Company, later Fieldcrest Cannon Incorporated and still later by other names.

In early 1992, a tall silver-colored marker was erected on U.S. 29 to honor the man who dreamed up and launched what became one of the textile industry's biggest success stories. The Kannapolis History Associates, members of the Cabarrus Bicentennial Commission and nearly one hundred other citizens and leaders gathered at the marker to view its unveiling. The marker was placed almost exactly on the city limits line shared by Kannapolis and Concord on U.S. 29, for Concord was Cannon's home, and Kannapolis, seven miles to the north, was his textile company's home.

The industrial genius of Jim's son Charles Cannon is generally considered the driving force of the company's national and international success through much of the twentieth century. But it was young Jim who thought it up, went through the nitty-gritty of fundraising and launched a complicated manufacturing operation.

Jim Cannon is credited with being the first to put his own brand name on woven material. He believed most people would remember goods if they carried a name—and that if they liked the goods, they'd come back for more.

Southern cotton mill owners once voted him tops in the Southern textile business over such mighty textile barons as Fuller Gallaway, Caesar Cone, Ellison Smythe, D.A. Tompkins, J.H. Montgomery and Lewis Parker. When he died in December 1921, Jim Cannon was

It was around 1907 that J.W. Cannon's dream came to fruition with the arrival of the first loom to go in his new mill. Those looms would weave his special terrycloth Cannon towels in those earliest years.

president and board chairman of, or otherwise actively involved with, the following companies: Cannon Manufacturing Company, with plants in Concord, Kannapolis and York, South Carolina; Cabarrus Cotton Mills, with plants in Concord and Kannapolis; Gibson Manufacturing Company in Concord; Franklin Cotton Mills in Concord; Patterson Manufacturing Company, China Grove; Kesler Manufacturing Company, Salisbury; Amazon Cotton Mills, Thomasville; Barringer Manufacturing Company, Rockwell; Efird Manufacturing Company, Albemarle; Wiscassett Mills Company, Albemarle; Tuscarora Cotton Mills, Mount Pleasant; Bloomfield Manufacturing Company, Social Circle, Georgia; Imperial Cotton Mills, Eatonton, Georgia; Buck Creek Cotton Mills, Siluria, Alabama.

In April, just before Jim Cannon's granddaughter, Mariam Cannon Hayes of Concord, helped unveil his marker, community and textile leaders had good things to say about "Mr. Jim." Robert Dellinger, a third-generation Cannon Mills employee now president of the bath division with Fieldcrest Cannon, pointed to Jim Cannon's first little four-thousand-spindle mill that grew into one of the largest manufacturers of home textiles in the world.

From the start, J.W. Cannon planned his new town, Kannapolis, to his specifications—mainly to build houses for his new textile workers. He also planned paved roads, streetlights and development of areas for businesses to serve their needs.

The 1908 YMCA was among the first buildings erected to serve Cannon's employees—and that it did, for nearly one hundred years. Provided was an endless list of activities—in community service, religious events, sports, ball games, swimming, movies, bowling alleys and more.

As Kannapolis grew, people began taking photos of the area—the first mill, the first YMCA and, of course, the dome-shaped lake with the small park at one end, where workers and families often gathered for band concerts or various meetings.

"Fifty percent of all towels sold in the United States today are Cannon towels," he told the crowd. "The Cannon name is among the most recognized in the world. Cannon is synonymous with the word towel."

Jim Cannon's prime business principle, wrote the *Salisbury* (North Carolina) *Evening Post* upon his death, was "Don't limit yourself. Pick out the biggest field you can find and the biggest goal in it and aim for it."

Cannon and Fetzer Store: First Step to Textile Fortune

Sunday, April 9, 2000

In downtown Concord at 21 Union Street: A Trading Company, go upstairs and you'll see a faint nineteenth-century store sign that figures big in the Cannon family fortunes. It's the fading old Cannon and Fetzer Store sign, painted on what was then an outside wall.

That store dominated the downtown for many years—later it was Belk, and today it's a shopping center with a variety of businesses, including a bakery. But in the late 1800s, Cannon and Fetzer was one of the more popular department stores in Concord.

Let's give thanks for old newspapers that printed these bits of history—and to all those dedicated amateur historians who clip and save the articles, which help preserve at least a portion of our heritage.

Anyway, in 1927 an unknown writer with considerable wit and fluency recalled much about those days. The article, first printed in the *Winston-Salem Journal*, was reprinted in a Concord paper. The writer believes that Jim Cannon's humongous fortune began with that local store. The headline begins the tale: "Old Cannon and Fetzer Store of Concord Was Foundation of Large Industrial Enterprizes in State."

The article began,

> *When bicycles were considered dangerous and silk stockings weren't even to be thought of; just after the passing of the hoop skirts and in the midst of the days of the bustle; not so long after Lee won a moral victory from the minions of the North and in the midst of the heroes of the "hard times," following this incident; there was being operated in the little village of Concord a store by Cannon and Fetzer.*
>
> *The Cannons were David and James W. The Fetzer was P.B.*
>
> *There wasn't anything so strange about that mercantile establishment. The usual things were sold there, which did not include automobile tires.*
>
> *But from this little store has grown one of the large private fortunes of North Carolina, the one built up by the late J.W. Cannon, and maintained by his heirs.*
>
> *The size of this fortune is not exactly known but it includes many cotton mills, and industrial enterprises, both in this and other states…*
>
> *The divers undertakings of the Cannon interest today, including many philanthropic and humanitarian tasks, are matters of public record and can be obtained in one way or another.*
>
> *But there are few living today who recall the days when Mr. Jim Cannon* [later multimillionaire] *used to walk in his store in*

Concord and help his clerks pacify an irate customer [It is supposed there were such things in those days] *to sell a pair of shoes.*

J.M. Lentz, Register of Deeds of Forsyth County, in his younger days used to clerk in the Cannons and Fetzer store, and was associated in other ways with the Cannon interests.

H.L. Cannon, now of Guilford College, was also a clerk in the establishment, which at one time was the trading center of Cabarrus, Stanly and adjoining counties.

[He] *remembers when the back lot adjacent to the Cannon store was filled with old covered wagons that had come from distant points to bring farm products and take back provisions.*

The erstwhile clerk remembers that the first bit of cement ever seen in Concord perhaps in North Carolina was laid down in front of the Cannons and Fetzer store.

It was the sensation of the times. People dropped down to the store in the afternoon to see this new kind of melted rock.

[That new concrete] *furnished food for the tete-a-tetes at luncheons.*

Finally Elam King, the richest man in Concord and consequently one whose judgment was not to be laughed at, gave the few feet of sidewalk close inspection and then remarked:

"Hmf. 'Twon't do. 'Twon't do. This sort of stuff might go in New York but it won't work in Concord."

But in spite of the dire augury made by Concord's plutocrat, the concrete sidewalks remained for the tramp of the feet of many customers.

And the concrete movement spread considerably.

$1.35 for Men's Shoes?

Sunday, April 16, 2000

Who was this witty writer on the Cannons? I guess we'll never know, but did he ever know all about the Cannons and Concord of the 1880s and 1890s.

"A good shoe could be bought in those hectic days for $1.35. This was the usual price.

"One time, a clerk got a badge of merit pinned on him for selling a pair of $5 shoes, and the man who bought the pair was generally credited with having more money than wisdom.

"The highest priced woman's shoe sold at Cannon and Fetzers retailed for $3.50, and a moderate price was $1.50.

"The most important thing about the lady's shoe was the tip end. Nothing else ever showed except in case of accident or high wind."

It's easy to savor the droll way our anonymous author put things.

"Everything was sold 'on time.'"

Sounds like our layaway today, but read on.

> Farmers came in the spring and stocked their store houses with such as they should need and then in the fall brought bales of cotton to the store along with farm produce and paid for goods purchased six months back.
>
> Cotton sold then for around four and five cents per pound. Other things raised on the farm were priced accordingly.
>
> Although Concord wasn't in the Metropolitan class, it had its city ways, such as livery stables. Much of the money spent by the young bucks of those days was spent on horses.
>
> A man that could slap the reins over a slick-backed roan that stepped like a thoroughbred was in the same class as a man who today drives a Tappan Eight or its equal. [A Tappan Eight? Whatever was that? Maybe an automobile.]
>
> There were always places to go, such as Rock Creek Camp Meeting or to the more distant hub of commerce, Charlotte.
>
> And then a drive on the wooded ways of Cabarrus County in company with a belle of the 1880s was not to be dispised [sic].

One former clerk the writer interviewed recalled that J.W. Cannon—who, with his brother David and P.B. Fetzer, owned and operated the store—was an "exceptionally good salesman."

He also "couldn't stand a loafing clerk," and when he'd walk in the store, "with a cough, any salesman who perhaps was engaged in a checker combat, would grab the nearest duster" and look very busy.

But J.W. Cannon was also generous, and his clerks stuck by him "in thick and thin."

The writer now tells how Jim Cannon once was fooled.

"A woman of hefty proportions came in for a pair of shoes. The later-to-become financial king waited on her and sold her a shiny black pair." She was pleased. So was he.

"There was a show in town that day, a big event," and the woman and her new shoes went to that show.

> *New shoes are not the most comfortable things in the world, and this was a hot day, and those leather casings got "het up," and so did the woman.*
>
> *A few hours after the sale, toting her shoes under one arm, she came snorting back to Mr. Cannon, and…accompanied with many embellishments, told him the shoes were too small.*
>
> *Mr. Cannon agreed with her and gave her a new pair. And it was all ended well.*
>
> *There were other things that happened such as might happen in any general store in the eighties and nineties, a fight, the sale of a man's pair of shoes to a woman who had a big foot and didn't know it, the sale of a bustle to the prettiest girl in Concord, a little gossip.*

The author tells what he knew about the third owner, P.B. Fetzer.

"Although not later becoming the capitalist that his partner in business did, he reared two boys, who became famous coaches at the University of North Carolina, and he was generally classed by his associates as being one of the best men ever born.

"And that is no mean achievement."

3.

Of Mud, Dust and Goods on Credit in 1920s Kannapolis

Sunday, April 23, 2000

As new mill town Kannapolis was growing up back in the 1920s, a young lad named Billy Workman, who later became a well-known newspaperman with the old *Daily Independent* newspaper, was growing up with it. Today Bill Workman is semi-retired, but he still writes a weekly column—usually about memories of those early days when Kannapolis was young. He also added some research that, combined with his own clear memories, makes for a fun, if unofficial, history of the town—also called the Towel City. "Mr. Cannon had to build houses, because the people coming in from farms to work in the mill had to have places to live," he recalled in a long-ago column.

"They came from close by. They came from the mountains. They came from South Carolina and Georgia"—especially from Madison County, Georgia, if many local records are correct.

In early years little Billy Workman attended North School. Later, Kannapolis old-timer Bill Workman, retired newsman, recalled with humor and nostalgia some of the early goings-on among young students and their strict teachers.

"A few came in motorized vehicles. Most came in wagons pulled by horses or mules. On those vehicles were piled furniture, a few groceries, wives and a lot of children." Those earliest mill workers were not just hard up, he wrote. "They were broke. They didn't even dream about building houses."

So Mr. J.W. Cannon got busy, in more ways than building dwellings. "Mr. Cannon [also] had to provide buildings in which merchants could sell things the mill employees had to have. The merchants' pockets were about as empty as the mill workers' pockets.

"It was all they could do to stock the stores they rented at dirt-cheap rates."

Alas, today, we've forgotten so much about those early times, those hard times.

"Compared to today's standards, that first mill was primitive," Workman wrote. "The early houses were primitive. The stores were primitive."

The stores, he continued,

> *were jot-'em-down stores in the truest sense. They sold groceries on credit, shoes and clothing on credit, coal on credit, furniture on credit. There were few cars, maybe one or two per street.*
>
> *We Workmans moved into a house on West Seventh Street while the carpenters were putting the hinges on the front door. It was like most houses in Kannapolis, except for a few downtown occupied by supervisors in the mills. Those houses were not much better. Our house sat on brick pillars. It wasn't underpinned. In winter, cold winds blew under it, over it and around it; in summer, hot winds blew under, over and around it. Some of the wind, hot and cold, blew through cracks and knotholes in the floor. A hall ran all the way through the middle of the house, with two rooms on each side of it. There were four in our family when we moved here—Mom, Dad, brother Bob and me. Sister Virginia came along later. To help make ends meet, Mom kept boarders. I remember one time when there were five boarders. Ten persons lived in that house and we didn't know we were crowded.*

Old-timer Vividly Recalls Growing Up

Sunday, May 7, 2000

Kannapolis's Bill Workman and his memories on growing up in the largest unincorporated town in the Southeast—home of Cannon Mills—combine lots of humor, some pathos and sometimes harsh reality.

And much of it centers on the Workman family's four-room mill house. He recalled:

> *Floors were covered with linoleum to help keep out the cold and the heat. It didn't work very well. In the summer the house got so hot the linoleum nearly melted. In winter, the cold made it brittle. We drove Dad up the wall by breaking off little chunks of the floor covering. There was one*

fireplace in a front room. At first, we depended on an open fire to keep us warm.

But as we began to go up the economic ladder, Dad bought a laundry heater that was supposed to radiate heat. He said it was an improvement, but I silently disagreed with him. We still burned up in front and froze behind. After a few years, Dad could afford a big heater that was supposed to radiate heat. It really wasn't much better. When the fire died, the house really got cold. Many mornings, the water in the bucket was solid ice, and Mom had to hammer and pick out chunks to make coffee.

"I detested the fireplace and heaters," Workman wrote. "It was my job to cut the kindling that Dad used to start the fire every morning and carry in five or six buckets of coal to keep the fire going from daybreak until bedtime." There were other inconveniences: "The house at that time had one electrical circuit. That was enough. At first, our only use for electricity was the burning of lights that dangled from the ceiling— one in each room. [Then] Mom went highbrow and bought an electric iron to replace the one she had been heating on the oil-burning cook stove. Dad took a bolder step and bought an electric fan. In time he acquired a radio. Drop cords were run all over the place."

Living in small quarters presented special problems, he recalled, especially when the family took in those five boarders. "A curtain was installed across the hall down the center of the house. Back of the curtain was where we Workmans and the boarders threw everything not needed at the moment." In later years, he continued, "Mom and Dad said that house on Seventh Street was the best one we had lived in up to that time. I guess they were right. I was only four years old when we moved here and don't remember the houses we lived in before."

The Cannon mill houses had at least one positive feature, Workman wrote:

It was certainly worth the rent. I remember the pay envelopes that Dad brought home back when Cannon [Mills] paid off in cash so the workers wouldn't have to bother with going to the only bank in *town. The deduction for rent was 75 cents every two weeks, and a few pennies more were taken out for electricity. That was fair enough: Dad made $18 every two weeks for 110 hours of work in the pipe shop.*

Dad was a good provider. After working 10 hours a day Monday through Friday and five hours on Saturday, he sold tailored-to-order suits. He made as much on this sideline as he did fitting pipe for Cannon. He was expert at trimming expenses. He put new soles on our shoes: A $2 pair could be resoled at least three times, at no more than a quarter a clip. He cut our hair; it took him an hour at least, but he saved a quarter a head. He made scooters, wagons, swings, seesaws and other playthings with junk he carried home from the mill. He worked a garden and kept chickens.

The years passed, and today Workman still enjoys walking or driving past his old haunts on West Seventh Street. He mused,

It's a different neighborhood. The houses are underpinned. They have been improved through the years and maintained well. Grass is growing where we never bothered to try to sow grass. Flowers are growing where Mom never had time to plant flowers. The trees are big. The street that I watched convicts build with picks and shovels and scoops pulled by mules, is now a wide ribbon of asphalt. The two-seat privies where people used to spend hours relaxing and scanning Sears and Montgomery Ward wish-books were replaced with inside bathrooms after we moved from the neighborhood in the mid-1930s. But I doubt that anybody ever enjoyed living on Seventh Street any more than I did.

In Early 1900s, School Principals Were "Lords"

Sunday, August 11, 1991

Do any of you think schools in Cabarrus County and probably elsewhere over the South a long time ago—say, 1925—were dull, lifeless, strict and not-so-hot places of learning?

Well, strict, yes—but how about little Bus Ford, a Kannapolis second-grader who drove an old Ford to school, standing up in the front seat to see where he was going, Bill Workman recalled.

He chuckled, recalling Matt King, who rode his pony to school every day—and let other kids ride it if they'd clean up after it. "Matt was our first cowboy at old North School—and Bus brought our first car to North School," he said. And nobody—not even principal or teachers—had a car at North School, except Bus.

Then he described a school principal who constantly stalked old North School halls, carrying a yardstick and a switch, looking for young offenders. "Those principals," Workman sighed, "they were lords. Bigger than God by far."

As you modern-day students, teachers, principals, school board members, administrators and parents begin another school year—perhaps grumbling about studies, grades, pay, hours and other shortcomings—look well on what might have been, if a capricious fate had thrust you into Bill Workman's Roaring Twenties.

Compared with school life as we know it today? "There's no comparison," Workman began. In 1925 kids walked to old North School, where at 8:00 a.m. the principal emerged, blew a whistle or rang a bell and the students lined up behind their teachers to hear instructions for the day. Then they marched behind their teachers into their classrooms, where they remained, except for a brief recess, until lunchtime. They walked home for lunch; cafeterias were unheard of. At 1:00 p.m. they lined up again for more instructions and marched back to class. At 3:30 p.m. school ended.

If they had learned well and behaved, they could leave, "but the teachers often kept us later," Workman said. "But it didn't matter. We didn't have anything else to do, and there were all those chores at home."

North School had no library. The indoor plumbing was brand-new. There was no playground equipment. "At recess, we just threw a ball around if we had one, or ran, or got in fights," Bill reported. But learning—basically readin', 'ritin' and 'rithmetic and a lot of history—was thorough and demanding, he recalled. "We also had to learn to sing 'The Old North State,' and we sang it every morning. We finally got an auditorium, and then we had chapel programs every morning."

There were always forty students in every classroom, and they sat in old-fashioned double desks. In 1925 the school year ran for six months. A year or two later it went to eight months and eventually to nine months. There were always a lot of "repeaters," he remembered, for teachers just didn't promote kids who didn't learn everything required for the year—like spelling fifty words a week and knowing the multiplication tables upside down and backward and forward.

"My fourth-grade teacher wasn't going to promote me because I hadn't learned the multiplication table—but she said if I learned it that summer, to come to her house and prove it. I did, and she promoted me. If you missed more than two spelling words a week, the teacher rolled your fingers back and hit them fifteen times with a ruler. It took about two rappings for me to decide it was best to learn them," he chuckled.

Every elementary grade had its high and low designation, he said, like low first grade and high first grade, high and low second grade. "The lows were usually the repeaters."

Was all this typical in area schools of that 1920s and '30s era? I can vouch personally for similar discipline and learning emphasis in Concord schools of the '30s. Who of the 1930s schools in Concord could ever forget Professor A.S. Webb at old Coltrane Grammar and Central Primary schools (now Coltrane-Webb Elementary)? Mr. Webb wasn't too hard on the girls, but ask any of the boys about his fair and heavy-handed discipline. And I'll never forget the paddlings that gentlemanly, cultured Brown McAllister (later superintendent of Concord City Schools) used to give our recalcitrant sixth-grade boys. I can even remember a little second-grade girl getting a switching that left red marks on her legs.

But back up to Bill Workman's old-time Kannapolis: After finishing the sixth grade at the old North School and South

School in Kannapolis—and maybe one other school there, Bill Workman recalled—students would go on to Cannon High School for grades seven to eleven. "I remember when we'd run away during the day, the principal, Mr. W.J. Bullock, always found it out and he'd track us down all over Kannapolis, even down into Petheltown, and drag us back to school.

"We'd sneak down the fire escapes and run across the campus, but he always found out and came looking for us."

No Fancy School Equipment, But Kids Were Good

Sunday, August 18, 1991

"Little" Billy Workman is still full of old-time memories from way back, and I'll add some research goodies from, say, sixty or so years ago—even a century ago.

In the late 1800s, all of Cabarrus County overflowed with many little schools for black students and white students, built where needed as transportation was about nil in those Depression-era schools.

Today's students and teachers read about those times with surprise and amusement...and maybe a little envy? Of course, old-timers will read of them with nostalgia.

"We didn't have much equipment at Cannon High back then," Little Billy said. "In the science lab, there were just a few tubes and burners and chemicals. Not too many books in the library." Media centers? Computers, videos, soccer and tennis teams? Are you kidding?

"But we had a good football team," he declared. "But we couldn't have but twelve players, because we didn't have but twelve uniforms. And when we played teams from out of town, we had to beg people to drive us there," he said. "We had to offer them a dollar for gas and tickets to the game to go play Statesville High School."

Discipline in those days continued to be world-class, he said. "The worse spanking I ever got was in the ninth grade. The teacher broke the paddle on me. I couldn't sit down for a couple days."

But you think the kids had it bad? Teachers in those days made perhaps sixty dollars a month, he said, "and not always that much."

In 1931, when W.J. Bullock—later Kannapolis's longtime and well-loved school superintendent—arrived to teach in Kannapolis, "he made $90 a month teaching, and $10 a month for being principal," Workman recalled. "Teachers! They were really at the mercy of the school board," he said.

Today it's hard to believe the near merciless, strait-laced attitudes he described. For not too many years back, Workman said, the women who taught had to be single. Those early school boards—most always composed of men—believed marriage changed women and, for some reason, rendered married women morally unfit to teach young children. (Surely this was because of the strong religious tenor, and the rigid sex mores and taboos of those times.) If a female teacher married, the school board immediately fired her.

"I remember one woman, who taught in Kannapolis and lived in Concord got married, and she kept it a secret for five years, so she wouldn't lose her job," Bill Workman said, with a laugh. "I also remember one time when a school board member came right into the classroom and fired the teacher, right in front of the class," he added. He didn't know what her offense had been. "He told the teacher to get her stuff together and get out, right then. I also remember that single Baptist women seemed to have the best chance of getting a teacher's job," Workman said.

However, all things considered, he said, "We took school more seriously in those days. We felt like we had to get all possible out of it, because each year might be our last. A lot of boys, some of them not more than twelve or fourteen years old, had to quit school to go to work in the mill, in those days.

"But in a lot of ways, it was better then," he mused—those days of hardworking, strict parents who threatened worse punishment at home if their young 'uns got in trouble at school. They were days without addictive drugs, days when if there was any student smoking, it was sneaked, because if you got caught, you were expelled. Those were the days when students didn't even think of drinking alcoholic beverages, much less bringing them to school.

A student owning a car was simply unheard of back then, which meant less aimless cruising around and less opportunity to get oneself into trouble.

4.

'30s Textile Strike: Bayonets, Tear Gas and Stabbings

Sunday, October 23, 1994

Date: September 1934.

Place: Cabarrus County, North Carolina.

Event: Bristling nationwide textile strike turned ugly, from Georgia to New England, with Cabarrus County smack in its midst.

Concord Tribune headlines trumpeted the violence, as did newspapers nationwide: "Blackjacks, tear gas, water hose and fixed bayonets were brought into play yesterday afternoon at Gibson Manufacturing Co., Cannon Plant No. 6 as the first riot of the textile strike here was quelled."

"Trooper stabbed by picket during riot" at Gibson Mill.

"Literally a library of Communistic literature was seized by Concord police officers with the arrest, at the home of Claude Clark on Dorland Avenue, of a woman who gave the name of Caroline Drew and her home address as New York City."

"Cheering was loud and sustained" at a midnight rally of four hundred strike sympathizers at Cabarrus Courthouse, and "strike enthusiasm was high" during remarks by L.R. Lawrence, president of the North Carolina Federation of Labor.

Kannapolis, Concord, all of Cabarrus County and textile cities everywhere were affected by the strike, for cotton was king and textiles the lifeblood in much of the nation. Nationwide, the United Textile Workers of America had ordered 725,000 workers to strike on September 1, but in North Carolina's Piedmont, many workers opposed it. Within a few days, four Concord plants—Buffalo, Roberta, Hartsell and Brown—closed because picketers kept most workers out. The first disturbance occurred early on at Hartsell Mill, where "Joe Bullard, striker, is alleged to have assaulted M.S. Gaskey with his fist" when Gaskey "insisted on going into the plant."

Oddly, in mill town Kannapolis, all was peace and quiet and work as Cannon Mills continued to run full force, with 100 percent worker attendance. Cannon Mills was a prime union target—but there was no picketing there yet. The *Tribune* wrote that "both sides are evidently intent on maintaining the peace," and mill owners assuredly "would close down plants to avoid trouble." It wasn't to last, but in those early days it seemed mostly like business as usual compared with the murder, assault, aggression, face-offs, dynamitings and other troubles that ran rampant throughout the textile world.

On September 5, President Roosevelt appointed a strike mediation board. That same day, picketers showed up at Cannon plants in Kannapolis, while in Concord, several hundred picketers showed up at Locke Cotton Mill (Locke Mill Plaza today).

Cabarrus Sheriff Ray Hoover quickly swore in one hundred special deputies. Concord Police Department similarly added to its force. Remember, nationwide strike violence had killed people from Georgia to Maine—seven in South Carolina—and National Guards and state militias were being called out, mills were dynamited and vigilante groups formed.

"You're going to start a revolution!" one striker was quoted as shouting to nonstrikers at a local plant. Union members and sympathizers in cars—"flying squadrons"—were reported as speeding from place to place, town to town, in lightning visits to various cotton mills.

The strike was essentially over money. The union wanted more money and fewer hours for its workers, establishment of maximum workloads and reinstatement of strike sympathizers. Hard-pressed mill owners, fighting the union and the Great Depression, said they couldn't stay in business if they met these demands. So the massive walkout continued.

Meanwhile, in Cabarrus, so many people were drawn to the picketed mills to see the excitement that county officials publicly asked them to leave. Law enforcement officers couldn't tell who were picketers, who were workers or who were spectators.

Then another fistfight erupted at Norcott Mill in Concord.

Picketers even marched at the old Kerr Bleachery, which wasn't involved in the strike but manufactured goods for Cannon Mills.

National Guardsmen, sent to keep order, were quartered at Mary Ella Hall in Kannapolis, and two of them rescued two youngsters from a stream, flooded by unusually heavy rains that week. The Guard, incidentally, had four machine guns among its pistols and rifles.

Morton Irvin, spokesman for an area strike committee, seemed indignant when he didn't know why the guard was sent to Cabarrus, as there was no "disorder" in the area. Irvin went even further, declaring local bootleggers were not being patronized by picketers and furthermore he knew nothing about any "flying squadrons."

By September 8, about 3,000 Cabarrus cotton mill workers were idled. Statewide, an estimated 63,000 mill hands were out; 52,000 were still working. At least 202 mills were closed, while 333 remained open. The union attack on Cannon Mills began in earnest September 10 when some 300 picketers from Salisbury and Mooresville flocked to Kannapolis.

In Boston that day, troops were called out to quell violence, and in Rhode Island things were so bad the state militia was called and federal troops were sent in. Even so, federal strike mediators reported, "The outlook is not hopeless." That likely didn't convince anybody down at old Plant 6 in Concord, where things turned really ugly.

Bloodshed at Gibson Mill

Sunday, November 13, 1994

The day shift hadn't left Gibson Manufacturing Company, Plant 6 on September 15, 1934, when rioting erupted and a National Guardsman was stabbed.

"Still the strikers surged about the gates and their ranks were not broken until tear gas bombs were hurled and mill hoses were turned on…Some of the bombs were picked up by the pickets and hurled back at the feet of the soldiers," local news accounts blared.

(I remember vividly when I was a nine-year-old child playing in the front yard of our home on North Union Street during this strike, hearing shouting up the street as cars loaded with men, hanging from windows and running boards, carried guns toward downtown. My father ran out about that time, picked me up and carried me in the house—to my disappointment.)

By then, the end of the tumultuous nationwide textile strike was still a week away.

"Sgt. Charles Fleming of the Statesville [National Guard] cavalry troop on strike duty here was the victim of a cowardly attack when he was knifed in the back by a man said to be between 60 and 65 years old," news clippings said.

"Fleming showed admirable restraint in checking an impulse to shoot down his assailant and, in the resultant confusion, the man made an escape through the crowd. He had not been arrested at a late hour this morning…The sergeant's wound was dressed in the mill office and he was later taken to the hospital here for observation."

The wound proved not to be serious—but the rioting was. "Patrolman Carl Honeycutt sustained several painful blows in the melee and several other officers are also nursing sore spots today…

One of the guardsmen had a bruised and bleeding forearm…Sheriff Ray Hoover, who took command when he reached the scene, ordered the arrest of four of the alleged leaders of the riot," three from Kannapolis, including a union official, and one from Concord. "They were still in jail at noon today, no bond having been set."

As many as four hundred strikers gathered at the mill gates that opened on public highways, and one group moved across the line drawn by guardsmen. As guardsmen pushed strikers back to clear the gates, Sergeant Fleming was stabbed.

"Within a few seconds the entire group was shouting defiance at the soldiers, whose ranks were soon augmented by comrades stationed at other mills and by special officers." The sheriff was booed when he arrived, but guardsmen and reinforcements "gradually drove the pickets back across an adjoining railroad track where they remained until news of the four arrests reached their ears.

"About a third of them then followed the sheriff and his prisoners to the county jail where they milled about for half an hour. Twenty special officers armed with shotguns prohibited them from getting on the jail property…Union men wanted to post bond for the men arrested."

Mill spokesmen told a reporter that an "erroneous rumor"—that a night shift was to go on duty at the plant—had brought the pickets to Plant 6's gates.

The incident ended nearly as quickly as it flared. By 10:00 p.m., "the city was quiet again…At the Gibson plant everything was normal." Well, the riot was the high point of the 1934 strike in Cabarrus County. Even in Kannapolis, where three hundred pickets once kept some workers out, Cannon Mills's plants continued to operate at some level. There was tension, but no violence.

A few books have been written and at least one video has been made on those violent three weeks in 1934. Nationwide, charges and countercharges flew between strikers and nonstrikers, unions and mill management, and the effects were deep, wide, far-reaching and long-lasting—and it would be impossible to address them all in a weekly column.

Cabarrus County's mill owners were hard-pressed to keep from shutting down during the Depression, which dropped the United States deeper into economic disaster. It lasted into the late 1930s. While many areas suffered economically, Cabarrus County seems to have survived in better shape than most, largely because of the strong textile industry here.

Cannon Mill managed to operate several days a week for most of the Depression—and it is significant that not one bank failed in Cabarrus County during the 1930s. It's also a matter of record that Charles Cannon, backed by his fortune, single-handedly saved the State of North Carolina from bankruptcy on one occasion.

Even so, Cabarrus had its share of joblessness, little money and lots of suffering and sacrifice.

That '34 strike embedded a deep distrust of government and unions alike, according to *Like A Family: The Making of a Southern Cotton Mill World*, written in the 1970s and published by the Fred Morrison Series in Southern Studies at the University of North Carolina.

A Kannapolis union officer wrote a letter at strike's end—September 22—to a national union official:

> *Our local is gone and it don't seem there is any use to try now as they have lost faith in the union. We have had so many promises and nothing done I myself am almost ready to give up...*
>
> *What is wrong[?] Have the whole works sold out...We as poor hungry people cannot live with[out] something to eat and something to wear to keep us warm.*
>
> *How do you people in Washington think we can go on living on air and promises. What we need is help and if you cannot get that for us then say so and we will not depend on promises any longer...*
>
> *It looks like Cannon Mills are running the whole thing. We want to know if they run the whole country it looks like it...*
>
> *Please...do something that we may be able to still have faith in our Government.*

One last tidbit for local memories: On September 7, 1934, Company E, Concord's crack National Guard unit, led by Captain Norman Alston, was dispatched to Kings Mountain on strike duty. Apparently the state felt it was best not to have local guardsmen confronting their local people.

5.

Old-time Football Rituals:
Kannapolis Versus Concord

Sunday, November 4, 1990

No one knows who'll be ringing the Victory Bell on Friday night, when Kannapolis's green-and-white elevens knock helmets with Concord's black-and-gold in the state's hottest football rivalry. This classic game is, of course, the Spiders versus the Wonders. This annual ritual will be as fraught with high spirits and other volatile emotions as it has from the beginning—dating back more years than a lot of us will admit.

Today's games are fascinating with cannon shots, players bounding through gaudy field-side tunnels, confetti, balloons, fireworks, nifty cheerleaders, big bands playing colorful marching numbers. The bands work for months, the A.L. Brown High Big Machine and the Concord High Marching Spiders, eager to wow each other as well as spectators. Cheerleaders perform routines we used to watch gymnasts and Fred Astaire do, with clever yells and rampant cheers.

Kannapolis's 1939 Cannon High School Band was the spiffiest in the whole of Cabarrus County with its bright green uniforms. It marched in local parades and played at local high school football games and other events.

At game's end, we hear the joyous ring of the Victory Bell and the sighs and sobs of the losers.

It wasn't always that way, folks. It doesn't mean they have a whit more fun or emotion today than we did half a century or more ago—say 1937, when I was in seventh grade in the Concord schools. There was no Victory Bell back then. The Wonders were called the Little Wonders, and Kannapolis had the biggest and best-uniformed high school band anywhere around these parts.

Football games, eagerly awaited in 1937, were played on Friday afternoons because there were no night lights. We had cheerleaders wearing full, longish skirts, thick sweaters, bobby socks and saddle shoes. They danced and shook their fists with yells like "Two, four, six, eight, who do we appreciate? Concord, Concord, Concord," among others. We had pep rallies in the auditorium to learn new cheers every fall.

Incidentally, Concord's Webb Field also was used by those 1930s professional "outlaw" baseball teams that Kannapolis and Concord fielded most summers through the Great Depression years—with intense competitions.

Anyway, after school, we'd run down to get a seat in the rickety wooden bleachers or the grandstand. Later, when lights were installed, we still went early for seats. I remember how some of those early night lights would explode with a shower of sparks in the chill night air.

We had bonfires, too, and parades downtown the day before, but not as many pregame pranks because in those days cars were not as available. After the games we had get-togethers, mainly at our homes, sometimes at a little cabin behind the residence of nearby Dr. Dick Rankin. Many a kid learned to do the big apple and jitterbug and fox trot at those postgame celebrations (whether we won or lost).

Kannapolis and Concord High Schools both played teams from Lexington, Thomasville and two orphanages, Barium Springs and Children's Home. The orphanages routinely whipped us every year. Our coaches said it was because the orphanages started their boys playing football in the first grade.

In 1937, we sat quietly at halftimes, watching that big, beautiful Kannapolis band and listening to their rooters' songs. At that time, Concord had only the frailest beginnings of a band—started by our math teacher, Mr. Kellogg. We hadn't learned much about marching, had no uniforms and worse, we didn't play so well those first years. But we showed 'em a couple of years later. Our Concord High School Band sported black wool sweaters with gold musical symbols on them as well as the CHS monogram. The boys wore them with white pants, the girls with white skirts. (Slacks were still taboo for girls.)

The Concord school board hired Mr. Curtis, a professional bandsman who trained and took us to band competitions at Richmond in 1940, where we earned a superior rating—the highest score in our category. Well, that set the community on fire. They bought millions of our doughnuts to help buy uniforms for our forty-eight band members. Finally, there we were, natty in full, handsome black-with-gold-trim uniforms. Girls wore black wool skirts.

The biggest thrill was yet to come—that big night at the Kannapolis-Concord game, at Kannapolis. I can't tell you what we played, the formations we marched at halftime that night or even who won the game. But I can tell you our beautiful band marched onto the field in those new uniforms, intermingling with the elegant green-and-white uniforms of the Kannapolis band, to play, as a massed band, "The Star-Spangled Banner." I'll bet our bandsmen will never forget how startled the Kannapolis band members looked when they saw us for the first time, in our CHS black-and-gold uniforms. Complete with two majorettes and a drum major, yet.

6.

Roy Rogers and Trigger at '40s Swanee Theatre

Sunday, June 26, 1994

It seems unlikely, but movie stars Roy Rogers and Trigger, along with Tex Ritter and Lash LaRue, all performed in person onstage at Kannapolis's old Swanee Theatre a long time ago. Now that historic Kannapolis building has become the Cannon Village Visitor Center. Where cowboys used to sing and play are now displayed two-thousand-year-old Egyptian textiles and hundreds of cotton mill items and artifacts from way back when. This fine museum of the textile industry history was created by Fieldcrest Cannon, Inc., and Cannon Village owner Atlantic American Properties, Inc., refurbishing and enhancing the Swanee. The colorful exhibits not only teem with Kannapolis history and textile processes, but the museum also presents compelling views of Fieldcrest Cannon's products, its aims and its future in dynamic fashion.

Early in World War II, 1942, the Swanee opened. America's Great Depression was ending and winning the war occupied minds, here and everywhere. During those hectic years and afterward, old-timers watched hit movies, World War II newsreels and live stage shows on the theater's big screen. And the Swanee became a place where people often met and mingled with their friends, for in those days, the movies were a dominant source of entertainment.

To accommodate the mill workers on all three shifts, the theater routinely scheduled its showings at 7:00 a.m., 3:00 p.m. and 11:00 p.m. In those years, Kannapolis residents were getting more hours of work, and thus more money to buy tickets to the Swanee. But thirty years and a lot of television later, the Swanee closed, in 1971.

But the old theater wasn't done yet. It was to rise again, of course, as the Visitor Center and later for the Cannon Village retail area in downtown Kannapolis.

Happily, the 1972 and 1990 remodelings preserved the old theater's architectural features: the elegantly curving walls, the lobby ceiling medallion, even the original stage. Rich in vintage Kannapolis photographs, the museum tells the Cannon Mills-Fieldcrest Cannon story in high-tech light, sound and color on the theater's original stage.

When you go, be sure to plan time for a leisurely tour to absorb its fascinating information. You'll see Cannon Mills founder J.W. Cannon in his office, featuring his desk and other turn-of-the-century items. Then you'll learn about Fieldcrest Mills's founder, Benjamin Franklin Mebane, and his great textile successes. Best of all, you'll catch much of the flavor of early Kannapolis and its people through mill artifacts, such as the original mill whistle from Cannon Mills Plant 2, the antique looms, vintage commemorative towels and the World's Largest Towel. Kannapolis old-timers will recall those deep, demanding whistles, growling or shrieking signaling the shift change times throughout the day.

The quite risqué advertisements on bed sheets, which you'll see in magazine ads of the 1930s and 1940s, may shock you a bit, as will the samples of Egyptian textiles at least 1,200 years old. You'll walk into the future with a touch-screen computer monitor that outlines modern textile manufacturing processes to end your tour.

In the one-hundred-seat theater, you can see a twenty-minute multi-image show flashed on a screen with music and narration. The entire Fieldcrest Cannon Textile Exhibition covers 4,500 square feet.

Historically, it seems fitting that Fieldcrest Cannon kept the new exhibition in the old Swanee. While time has changed Kannapolis, Fieldcrest Cannon and Atlantic American Textile Museum has managed to retain a large part of the mill heritage for everyone to see, every day.

7.

War Empties Dugouts, But Local Lawyer
Saves Baseball

Sunday, August 5, 2001

Kannapolis and Concord have long been dubbed historical hotbeds of baseball, with rivalries as explosive as firecrackers between these sister cities. Nearly six decades ago, however, World War II was taking its toll on the military, on citizens on the homefront and on professional sports.

All sports were losing talented players, as more and more able-bodied men, including professional athletes, enlisted or were being drafted into military service. By 1943, baseball dugouts were rapidly emptying here and across America. In 1941, for example, forty-one professional baseball teams were in operation in the area. A year later, there were thirty-one. In 1943, only ten pro teams were playing.

Among the baseball casualties that year, reports Hank Utley, who wrote a book on baseball here with Scott Verner, was the Class D

Kannapolis always was a baseball happy town with its own team, the Towelers, which competed with teams all around the area—but with particular vigor against the hottest rival, nearby Concord's Weavers. Bill Whitley was owner.

North Carolina State League, which included Concord's Weavers and teams from Mooresville, Thomasville, Landis, Lexington, Statesville, Salisbury and Hickory—and for a short time, Kannapolis's Towelers. Oh yes, Kannapolis had a team in those days, but Cannon Mills's dedication to the war effort resulted in withdrawal of the Towel City Nine from play in those years.

Utley's latest report, "Summer of 1943 in North Carolina—War Time Textile Town Baseball—the Best and the Worst," will give you some hearty laughs from the small-town wartime:

> *It appeared that if these textile towns in piedmont North Carolina were to have any baseball in 1943 it would be semi-pro mill teams playing each other within one town's geographical area.*

However, one man, [Concord's] C. Manley Llewellyn [respected lawyer and former judge], *who had been president of the N.C. State league for four years, stepped forth to give guidance and leadership to this historical hotbed of baseball.*

As president of the now defunct N.C. State league, he encouraged these small textile towns to organize town semi-pro teams that would play close by neighboring towns.

Thus was born the Carolina Victory League, semi-pro baseball at its best during wartime restrictions but at its worst with typical textile town intrigue, fighting, gambling and plain ol' baseball cheatin'.

Forming the league wouldn't be easy, but Llewellyn was up to the task. He was a big, muscular man endowed with rich humor, a quick-witted lawyer who settled into his practice after playing briefly for the New York Yankees in the early 1920s.

"I want to see baseball continue in the communities of our N.C. State League this season," said "Mr. Lew," as he was called by many friends, "despite the fact that we were forced to close shop. It was impossible for our clubs to continue this year due mainly to the player shortage. But that doesn't mean necessarily that baseball in our cities must cease for the duration" of the war.

People, he continued, "want baseball this year, probably more than ever because a few hours of relaxation and recreation come in handy after a hard day's work."

It would "mean much to the smaller cities during wartime. It will keep alive the sport for both the players and spectators, and the use of the lights at Webb Field for night games will tend to elevate the game to professional style," Mr. Lew was quoted as saying.

In 1943, playing baseball at night was still quite new and exciting to local fans. That year, Llewellyn had "started the ball rolling toward a compact, semi-pro baseball league (made up of aged professional veterans and youngsters) that would give the Piedmont North Carolina home front needed recreation in the midst of ever increasing casualty and war death notices from the fighting front."

A real highlight: this little league produced a future Major League star, Concord native Billy Goodman. Goodman, who was seventeen when he played in the Carolina Victory League, won the 1950 American League batting title while playing for the Boston Red Sox. Well, 1943 was to be a memorable summer, with fights, questionable umpiring and other hijinks.

Major Leagues Steal Local Players

Sunday, August 26, 2001

Professional baseball everywhere was hurting that summer of 1943. "Professional baseball scouts [for Major and minor leagues] were beginning to comb the Carolina Victory League," Utley wrote.

Big league scouts caused near-riots by trying to sign the local players on the spot, including during games.

Utley wrote, "Don Harwood, American Legion star from Albemarle and member of the Concord Weavers, was pitching a no-hitter against the Salisbury Aggies, when Claude Dietrich [scout for the Atlanta Crackers, one step below the Major Leagues] called him aside during the fourth inning and tried to persuade him to sign then and there.

"After [Harwood] returned to the mound, Jim Mallory, Salisbury outfielder [and former UNC star and Washington Senators player and currently a Catawba College coach] homered to start a five-run rally for Salisbury that won the game.

"Concord's manager, Ginger Watts, was furious over the bloodhound's inopportune tactics.

"Sam Swartz, general manager of the Salisbury Aggies, also hit the ceiling when Dietrich tried to talk to his players while a game was being played. Swartz called Atlanta," reporting the incident, and officials there promised to stop the behavior.

Ira Thomas, longtime Philadelphia Athletics scout, once invited local player Red Ennis to Philadelphia for a workout with the A's—baseball great Connie Mack's team—but Ennis said no. Ennis later signed with the Boston Red Sox. Actually, Utley wrote, Dietrich's prize catch was local baseball great Billy Goodman, who was playing with the Atlanta Crackers. When he won the American League batting crown in 1950, his average was .354.

If all that wasn't enough, real problems erupted among fans, players and sportswriters over umpiring, Utley wrote. League president Mr. Lew could hardly keep umpires at the games, what with wartime gas rationing and the umps' irregular working hours. Sometimes umpires simply didn't show up.

A *Salisbury Post* sportswriter stated, "It shouldn't be news to [Llewellyn] that fans are more than a little dissatisfied at the handling of the umpire situation and are demanding that something should be done.

"For some time now, games at Salisbury have been run by one league umpire, with a player or two from the competing teams filling in where there should be another 'blue suit' with eyes.

"It always makes players serving as umps look bad when they have to call a close play against their own team," the article continued.

In fact, one ump hadn't shown up in so long, the article claimed, "You'd think the prexy [president] would realize that he'd quit."

The Dingler brothers, a pair of local umpires, came in for special criticism: "It did not take much imagination on the part of fans to change their name to 'Dingbats.'" Another, Ed Cross, had a son on the Landis team and umpired a lot of Landis's games.

"Of course Ed no doubt was calling 'em like he saw 'em, regardless who was affected, but that didn't keep the bleacher wags from saying Ed had turned over a new leaf and decided to be honest about the whole thing," the article continued.

"But lousy umpiring just irritates the customers so much they can't enjoy the games, and they finally get in the habit of staying at home and reading the papers, where they can get just as mad at John L. Lewis and Hitler without buying a ticket or burning rationed gas," the *Post* item concluded.

"With problems like this," Utley asked, "why would C. Manley Llewellyn love this game?

"It could be that the Victory League was doing just what Lew wanted it to do—supplying good family entertainment with a lot of hullaballoo that temporarily diverted their attention away from the war."

Comic Ballplayer Swartz Tickled Fans and Irked Umpires

Sunday, September 2, 2001

By July 1, 1943, the main problems of the Carolina Victory Baseball League were solved. One of the ridiculed umpiring Dingler brothers—nicknamed Dingbat, of course—had resigned and fled to Akron, Ohio, to call baseball games there.

President Llewellyn raised the league's monthly dues from $27.50 to $30, and an all-star team was being chosen to play the Navy Pre-Flight School team based in Greensboro, which featured Boston Red Sox stars Ted Williams and Johnny Pesky, who were then in the military.

With all the hijinks, it was the Salisbury Aggies, last in the standings, who were tops in the entertaining in the league that included teams from Concord, Charlotte's Highland Park Mills and Landis.

Utley quoted a Concord newspaper article, which stated, "The Aggie general manager, Sam Swartz [who had helped fund the Aggies], was keeping everybody loose with his antics" on and off the diamond.

Added sportswriter Fred Severance:

"When his players ran to the Salisbury dugout to take their first turn at bat, the swarthy Swartz would proceed as though wound up like a mechanical toy in the other direction. His face reminded us of Charlie Chaplin, with a mustache to match. He would return to the bench with a walk suggestive of Donald Duck. If he faced a Concord player, his mustache would lift almost imperceptibly, and a word or two of greeting would follow."

Bleacherites loved Sam:

> *As he passed by, one of them would say, "Get in there and pitch, Sam. You can hypnotize the sluggers with your mustache."*
>
> *We could see that this fellow Sam had scored a bull's eye with the bleacherites. If his flinger [pitcher] shows signs of falling apart, Sir Samuel, with a shifty glance at the umpire, will enter the sacred precincts of the infield like a dancer leading the grand march.*
>
> *A hush descends as the First Citizen of Salisbury approaches his luckless pitcher, gesticulating and waving his arms like Don Quixote's windmill.*
>
> *He evidently wants to relieve the hapless pitcher in the box, but the southpaw won't surrender the ball and grips it tightly amidst the howls of delight* [from the fans].
>
> *The one-man comedy is a hit with all except the umpires, who eye the star performer icily from afar.*

Swartz then gave the unfortunate pitcher a "Red Grange push" (referring to the famous football running back).

Sam had far-flung ideas about the boundaries of the strike zone, the article continued.

And the umps? When Sam approaches, "They reach for their gas masks as though they had served in World War I."

Dissatisfied, Sam "led the charge—minus his bayonet—to the box seat of Prexy [president] Llewellyn," where they talked for 10 minutes, "Llewellyn looking at the sky, Swartz quivering with impatience."

Much to Sam's annoyance, the game went on. He gave the umpire and the crowd the "V for Victory" sign.

"Fans know that he had just begun to fight."

The Victory League all-stars played Navy Pre-Flight and its big-leaguers on July 17, 1943. The big boys, of course, mauled the locals, 11 to 3, Utley wrote. But it's not too discouraging to get beaten by the likes of Williams, Pesky, Harry Craft of the Cincinnati Reds and Buddy Hassett of the New York Yankees.

Some of the excitement of that big game had evaporated the day before, when "all hell broke loose" at a meeting of Victory League officials.

Llewellyn read his statement, "I am suspending Sam Swartz for the remainder of the season on account of conduct and attitude detrimental to baseball."

The "detrimental" part was a cardinal sin of baseball—gambling on the outcome of games.

"Swartz immediately appealed. The precarious life of this wartime semipro league was in real danger," Utley wrote.

Reaction of the league board was mixed: two supported Llewellyn, but Red Ennis disagreed.

Then Swartz declared he wouldn't let anyone else play on his baseball field. The Aggies players said they wouldn't play for anyone else. "After this news, Llewellyn stated, 'I don't know just what will happen to the league.'

"I think it would be better" for the league to fold than to allow such antics to continue at games, Llewellyn wrote in his statement.

Victory League's Aim: Escape from War Worries

Sunday, September 23, 2001

You can imagine how angry comical Sam Swartz was over his suspension as general manager of the Salisbury team.

"Swartz said he had lost about $1,000 of his own money, but that he had split the winnings with his players because game gate receipts were poor," wrote Utley.

Swartz was accused of betting on the team's games—detrimental to baseball, declared President Llewellyn.

The Victory League's extra "entertainment" continued to be highlighted that wartime summer, but it came with player fights, umpire-baiting, big league scouts still recruiting locals and Swartz's comic antics on the field—that is, until a Charlotte sportswriter blew the betting whistle on Sam. "I was railroaded," Swartz retorted. He said he split his winnings with players, that the boys, in effect, were playing just for the fun of it. Also, Swartz had riled the Catawba College baseball coach over plans to take his college students to try out for Connie Mack's Philadelphia Athletics—canceling several league games in order to do it.

The league expanded a bit in late summer when the Mooresville Moors, managed by Johnnie Hicks, joined. And a gargantuan home run was hit by Concord Weaver Norman Small, formerly with Mooresville and a minor league home run hero. An awed area sportswriter reported, "Lost: one baseball. Last seen over the left field fence at Webb Field Thursday night, the destination appeared to be North Union or Church Street. P.S. It was the homer hit by Norman Small."

Concord's North Union Street, incidentally, is three blocks from Webb Field and Church is four. In fact, Small "literally tore up" league pitchers before he left to join the army in August, Utley wrote.

The scramble for players continued into late summer, as players quit because they couldn't find gas to drive to games, or they were taking vacations or joining the military. And league all-stars got whupped again by those big-league players in wartime training at Chapel Hill on August 1.

But for fans and players, there was a compensation in the loss: all-star pitchers—Dick Mauney, Virgil "Coddle Creek" Taylor and Red Ennis—held Major League Hall of Famer Ted Williams hitless in four at-bats.

That, wrote Utley, "was something to remember."

Well, the season ended August 14, but the fireworks didn't. During the Concord-Landis playoffs, Concord claimed that Landis had used an ineligible player, Roy Pinkston, who had jumped a contract with Rochester, New York, in the International League. Pinkston argued he didn't know he was ineligible because he was not notified of that fact until August 21. A league inquiry followed. Utley wrote, "Judge W.G. Bramham, czar of organized professional baseball, replied that Pinkston had not been notified of his ineligibility until Saturday, Aug. 21, so he was eligible to play for Landis until that time." Llewellyn agreed. The dates of notification made Pinkston "within his rights signing with Landis."

Landis then accused the Weavers of using two ineligible players: Norman and Dub Johnson. Here's how Salisbury sportswriter Bill Peeler tried to straighten it all out, Utley wrote: Briefly, Peeler concluded that notification dates cleared Pinkston, and Concord also came out OK, sort of. Concord had used two unsigned players, Small and Johnson, who returned to Concord while on furlough from the army, but they were re-signed by the Weavers before the playoffs—and Concord also had used more than the allowed eighteen men per team.

Well, Llewellyn threw this jumble of things to the league's board of directors. Meanwhile, Highland Park (Charlotte) players griped that if an amicable agreement couldn't be reached quickly, they'd stop their season with no playoff finals.

The league board's vote ruled that both Concord and Landis teams broke the rules, but as Landis won the series, four games to one, the games would stand as played. At season's end, Concord sportswriter Roy Christenbury wrote, "Lew [Llewellyn] has had a hard job" from start to finish. "We must say, 'He's done OK.'"

In the end, Highland Park won it all on September 2, beating Landis four games to three. Days later Utley wrote, "On Sept. 8, the Italian government surrendered to the Allies, but there would be many months of bloody fighting before the world would return to peace." And little mill town baseball could finally "join the peaceful National Association of Professional Baseball Leagues"— the organized minor leagues.

Maybe our 1943 philosopher got it just right: the Victory League, with all its fights and antics, did help take local Americans' minds off World War II.

8.

Twenty Highway Markers Tell History of Kannapolis and Cabarrus

Sunday, May 27, 2001

Bet most of you can't name all the historical markers that dot Cabarrus County. Don't worry: most people couldn't.

There are twenty of the tall black-and-silver signs along Cabarrus highways now, pointing to significant local historical events, places and people from a seventeenth-century Indian trading path to a marker dedicated to twentieth-century textile magnate Charles A. Cannon. The markers are scattered throughout the county—one in the extreme northeast corner, three in Kannapolis, two in western Cabarrus, two in the Harrisburg vicinity, six in the Concord area, one in mid-Cabarrus, four in the Mount Pleasant area and one in southern Cabarrus near Midland.

Now let's take a look at each, noting that Cabarrus's interest in marking things historic began in 1936, when two markers were installed along county roads.

Granville Grant: Half of North Carolina was granted to Lord Granville by the English king in the seventeenth century. The southern grant line runs east-west through Kannapolis.

James W. Cannon: Mr. J.W., born in 1852, founded Cannon Mills Company. He died in 1921.

Charles A. Cannon: Son of Mr. J.W., Charles Cannon advanced Cannon Mills's operations to international levels through his business acumen. Born in 1892, he died in 1971.

Warren Coleman: Born a slave in 1849, Coleman made U.S. history as the first African American man to establish and run a successful textile mill operated by an all-black staff. He died in 1904.

Jefferson Davis: President of the Confederate States of America, Davis spent the night of April 18, 1865, at a home near downtown Concord. He and his cabinet were fleeing Federal troops near the Civil War's end.

Trading Path: This historic north-south trading route along the eastern seaboard cut through Cabarrus County. It was first used by Native Americans, white explorers and settlers in the seventeenth century. It extended from southern Virginia to the lands of North Carolina's Catawbas and Waxhaws.

W.R. Odell: A complex man—textile manufacturer, state senator, friend of education—Odell lived in a mansion on Union Street North, Concord, which is no longer standing.

James P. Cook: Another multitalented man, Cook was instrumental in founding Stonewall Jackson Training School (now Stonewall Jackson Youth Academy). He also was a state senator and editor of a local newspaper.

Stonewall Jackson Training School: This was the state's first home and school for boys, opened in 1909 near North Carolina Highway 49. Boys were taught agricultural and manual training.

Mill Hill: Built around 1821 by Jacob Stirewalt, this handsome old home near Kannapolis is an early example of Greek Revival architecture in the South. In its heyday, the estate was almost a full village, with stores, a mill, a post office and other facilities.

Red Hill: This colonial tavern and residence was visited by President George Washington in 1791. Probably the county's most historic relic, it was torn down. However, some pictures of it still exist.

It's Not Hard to Erect Historical Markers

Sunday, June 3, 2001

It isn't complicated to apply for a North Carolina highway marker raised for a favorite historic person, site or event, state authorities say. Compile all pertinent information, with documentation, if needed. Then call a North Carolina Department of Transportation office.

The remaining markers in Cabarrus County are:

Israel Pickens: Born in the Odell area west of Kannapolis, Israel Pickens was a congressman and U.S. senator from North Carolina. He moved to Alabama, where he became its first governor, 1821–1825.

Nathaniel Alexander: Born on what is now Lowe's Motor Speedway land, Dr. Nathaniel Alexander served as North Carolina governor from 1805 to 1807. Prior to that, Alexander was a surgeon during the Revolutionary War. His birthplace has been torn down.

Rocky River Presbyterian Church: The oldest Presbyterian church in several surrounding counties, Rocky River Church this year celebrated its 250th anniversary It was led in colonial days by firebrand preachers who supported the colonies' freedom from England, even before the Revolution. The present church was finished in 1860.

St. John's Lutheran Church: Six years older than Rocky River Church, St. John's was founded in 1745 and its members lived, farmed and fought through the same historic periods as did other area settlers. The earliest building, still standing, went up in 1845, three hundred yards north of the church.

Mont Amoena Seminary: This Lutheran school educated young girls from 1859 to 1927. Its name is Latin for "Mount Pleasant."

Mount Pleasant Collegiate Institute: A junior college for young men, it began as North Carolina College from 1853 to 1902, then changed to its current name. It closed in 1933.

Samuel Suther: The Reverend Samuel Suther, among the earliest ministers of the German Reformed Church, preached at Coldwater Union Church.

Bethel United Church of Christ: This church also formed in 1745 as Dutch Buffalo Creek Church. The church practiced the German Reformed and, later, Lutheran faiths from 1806 to 1875. The present structure was finished in 1929.

Reed Gold Mine: The site of the first gold rush in the United States, Reed Mine resulted from a boy's discovery of a gold nugget there in 1799. On news of the Reed find, people rushed to the area and many other gold mines were subsequently discovered. Reed, noted for its large nuggets, furnished much of the nation's gold until 1849, when the California rush began.

To be awarded a highway marker, the subject or site must be of considerable significance, a state official said. A formal written request must be filed and the final decision on each is up to NCDOT officials. The entire process, from request to approval to making and installing the marker, takes about three months.

9.

Trim, the Big Mule, Helped
Build Kannapolis in 1906

Sunday, June 1, 2003

We have a fun story for you about a big black mule and 1906 pre-Kannapolis. Trim the mule, a remarkable if stubborn beast, helped launch Kannapolis back when the Towel City was still just a country field in north Cabarrus County. The first day of construction was November 20, 1906, recalled Trim's owner, W.E. Bostian of China Grove. Trim, about seven, was vigorously earning her keep and more.

All of this comes from a news story in the *Cannon News*, which first appeared in the old *Kannapolis Daily Independent* in 1934.

Trim's story "sheds light on a factor often overlooked by others: The unseen power that made the work [of building Kannapolis] possible."

Old Trim and her mule cohort "hauled in the first load of lumber that started Kannapolis," Bostian reported to the Kannapolis paper. "Captain Price was [construction] superintendent, and Walter Dayvault, Mr. Simpson and Mr. Noval were the three carpenters who were then employed." Furthermore, the four "were present when the lumber was unloaded near an old gum tree where Mill No. 2 now stands."

That first load contained twelve hundred feet of green lumber, but later loads were fifteen hundred feet, "hauled over the old dirt road between what is now Kannapolis and China Grove. There was no paving to ease the loads pulled by the team. During the hauling of lumber, old Trim and her mate broke down two wagons and a new one with three-inch spindles. The one used to finish hauling the lumber had 3¼-inch spindles." A spindle is part of a wagon's axle. Spindles that size were especially hefty.

Old Trim's working prime seemed to last forever, owner Bostian revealed. "In her prime, old Trim could walk from China Grove to Salisbury or Concord in one hour, and was a fast trotter. She was never known to be overloaded," and, in fact, she had literally "worked out [out-worked?] two mules of her weight.

"One would think that after a life of such activity Trim [foaled in 1899] would be on the retired list, but she is still going strong and from all appearances is not about to rest," the 1934 article claimed.

For thirty years, Trim and her owner were "factors in the growth of Kannapolis; as recently as 1933 old Trim was hauling through Kannapolis the shaft that bored several wells" in the city, the article continued. At thirty-five years old—a remarkable age for a mule—she weighed thirteen hundred pounds "and has never been disabled a day since I bought her over 30 years ago," Bostian claimed.

Well, hard worker that she was, old Trim finally exhibited one eccentricity: "Strange as it may seem, on New Year's Day of 1934, this old mule decided for some reason or other that she was not going to have the bridle on her. Although well advanced in years, she asserted her rights, and it required the combined efforts of both Mr. and Mrs. Bostian to bridle Trim."

Trim, in her dotage, was much loved. "She has become so valued a part of the Bostian estate that she is being kept for 'old time's sake.'" Even better, the public was invited to come see her at any time at the Bostian home. She passed on to her reward at thirty-seven years, probably happily unaware that her laborious years helped build Kannapolis.

10.

Humor Rampant in Way-Back-When Letter

Sunday, July 20, 2003

People, I'd give my eyeteeth and other valuables to know who sent me this nigh-comic country letter, with more about old Trim, Kannapolis's favorite mule—and more. Not only does this letter tell us a little more about that lovable black mule, but it also gives us a vivid picture of country life around Kannapolis and southern Rowan way back when. The letter was written in large type, well spaced, cleanly printed. But the envelope has no return address, and the letter is unsigned—and, like old Trim, it packs a wallop in more ways than one. The letter was dated June 2, 2003:

> *Greetings I read your little story in the Observer about "Trim, the Mule that helped build Kannapolis."*
>
> *I am not very smart. But I can remember Old Trim walking around that shaft. Rig? as Will Bostian bored a well in our back yard.*

Will Bostian was the brother of Frank, who was the Daddy of Dean A., who was married to my Daddy's sister also a Bostian.

Are we confused?

Will lived on Bostian Road in China Grove at Hwy 29. Hwy 29 was not there at that time. But seem like another road was. I was only a few years old.

Will had a old REO truck [Oldsmobile] *with wood spokes wheels and solid rubber tires body was wood Will called it his "Furniture." He haul the Well boring shaft on it and his tools.*

Trim walked around the rig turning the shaft, bringing the dirt out of the well. Then Will would lower the pipe in the hole after they struck or got water.

Will's Daddy, Lawson, died in 1935. Took him to church for the funeral and burying.

It was said that he had money hid at home. Before they got the grave covered, His nephews were back looking for the money with their suit coats still on.

Dug all the manure out of the barn.

My Grand Daddy, not a Bostian, sawed and hauled lumber to help build the mills.

Will's brother Frank drilled wells. Had a machine with a gas motor that turned the drilling bit.

[Brother Frank also] *had old Brown Chevrolet car. He pulled the machine from place to place, hauled his cigars and Liquor in it.*

Had to smoke a box of cigars and drank a bottle of Liquor every day to be able to run the well machine.

Drilling a well at A. T. Allen School back when it was built, on Hwy 601 below Concord and "Lost the Tools in the Hole."

My Daddy's uncle was a Preacher and a blacksmith. So Frank went to him to make a piece of something that Frank thought might be able to get the tools out of the hole.

After some doings, Daddy's Uncle and Frank got the Tools out. Frank offered the Preacher a cigar and a drink of Liquor. Can't remember what Frank told the Preacher.

Daddy only got about a third grade education, attended a two room school with pot belly stoves and two hole outhouse out back. So did I the first year I went to school.

The rest of this humorous letter is just as appealing.

Trim Again, Plus Country Cousins and a Dying Cemetery

Sunday, July 27, 2003

A bit of unfinished business before we get back to our anonymous letter writer—because of a century-and-a-half-old graveyard switch.

I extracted an item about the Presbyterian and Lutheran cemeteries in Concord, from the final edition of the 1857 *Concord Weekly Gazette*.

Seems that editor James Henderson, in describing what then were the only two graveyards in Concord—the Presbyterian and Lutheran cemeteries—was scolding the Presbyterians for letting cattle roam amid their cemetery's graves, as well as its run-down condition.

As to the Lutheran burying ground nearby, he termed it "tolerably well kept."

Well, what a complete switch nearly 150 years can make.

I walked through that old Lutheran cemetery the other day, where some important early Concord and Cabarrus County folk rest in peace—including a general from the War of 1812. There were weeds everywhere, tree limbs, broken tombstones, turned-over grave markers, snaky-looking underbrush everywhere.

Then I thought of the historic Presbyterian cemetery, just blocks away, and a jewel now known as Memorial Garden. It has been a secluded haven of beauty in downtown Concord since the 1950s. Now how is that for a complete switch for two cemeteries? There's been talk of restoring the rundown Lutheran graveyard. I'll keep you posted.

81

Now, back to the droll, salty, unsigned letter, regaling us with tales of those old-time golden days around here. He or she wrote:

Daddy wanted me to have it better than what he had. He sent me off to a school up in Virginia. I wis[h]ed he had never done that.

When he sent me off, some of the kinfolks thought there was something wrong with me.

Most still do. I just ignore them.

My great-granddaddy's daddy was killed at Gettysburg on July 3, 1863. The last day of the battle, and Great-Granddaddy on my daddy's mama's side of the family was with him, and he was wounded in the back.

Don't know how much schooling my great grand had. After he grew up and got married, he farmed like most every body.

In the fall after selling the cotton, he would buy new pair of blue stripe bib overalls. They had a paper label on the right back pocket.

He wouldn't wash them until he got the next new pair so people would think he always had on a new pair of overalls when he went to Kannapolis.

Every Saturday morning he would hook his horse to the buggy, put on his overalls and black derby hat and go to Kannapolis and talk with other farmers that come in.

Was telling about his chickens having the mites; someone told him to take the chickens out of the chicken house, sprinkle some straw on the floor and set the straw afire. That would kill the chicken mites.

When he got home, he hurriedly got the chickens out. One really messed on his bib overalls.

After sprinkling the straw and setting it afire, he burned down his chicken house.

Had to wash his overalls and put up his horse.

They say that was the only time in 91 years that he ever said a bad word.

Mr. Letter Writer, whoever you are, how about some more of your droll memories?

And They Thought Great-Granddaddy Was a Ghost!

Sunday, August 3, 2003

Praise be! I got my wish.

Another unsigned letter arrived from the witty old-timer who recollected so much about that old Kannapolis mule, Trim, and lots more around the Kannapolis area.

This time, our penman remembers Korea, a pie safe, a country ham bowl and sixteen-ounce Pepsis, writing, "Today is the 50ᵗʰ anniversary of the signing of the armistice that ended the fighting in Korea. I was there and always remember. Our rifle company was on an outpost out in front of the main line.

"We were one more happy bunch of people at 10 p.m. that night."

Now meet Great-Granddaddy,

> *My Great-Granddaddy was called W.D., and his wife was Lizzie* [Elizabeth]. *Their house was built like the Duke Homestead over in Durham.*
>
> *They had a brick pie-baking oven outside the house. On Fridays they would bake pies for the next week: sweet potato, apple and any other fruits.*
>
> *On W.D.'s trip to Kannapolis on Saturday he would re-supply his little brown bags of different candies.*
>
> *W.D.'s was one place I was always ready to go. The pie safe was full. So was the country ham bowl. I have that bowl.*
>
> *But* [I] *knew the limit was only one piece of candy. Had to act my very best or I may not get that one piece of candy.*
>
> *W.D. went with two daughters on the train to California to visit relatives. Took over a week one way.*
>
> *When they got back, after picking them up at train station, Granddaddy, Daddy and an uncle was going to the coast fishing.*
>
> *W.D. said if they had any room for him, he would like to go along. They left after milking the cow.*

W.D. had asthma. Carried some kind of powder, a small bowl and a 36-inch square of white cloth with him in case of attack.

Off to the coast. It was after the sun went down. They were in a big four-door Dodge car. Back then, the highways were narrow and curvy; 25-30 miles an hour was about all you could do.

They were on the other side of Southern Pines about 1 a.m. when W.D. had an asthma attack.

Pulled over off the road, turned the overhead ceiling light on, and W.D. was on the back seat with white cloth over his head. Lit the powder and smoke was pouring out, filling the car.

The fishermen were standing in the field on the right side (remember, it was pitch dark).

A car came down the road and stopped beside the Dodge. Whoever it was set there a good minute, put their car in low gear, the pedal to the metal, and away they went, never changing gear as long as the fishermen could hear their car.

Was W.D. a ghost?

The fishermen went on their way after W.D. recovered and took the white cloth off his head and extinguished the burning powder.

Runaway Model T: The Barnyard Fun Just Doesn't Stop

Sunday, August 17, 2003

I'm not really sure how to do it, but today I want an old Model T Ford and the historic old Lutheran cemetery in Concord to meld into one column. Judge Clarence Horton, recognized as an expert local historian, has written a nostalgic piece on that old Lutheran burying ground in Concord and its many local historic people who lie there.

But our country cousin, up around southern Rowan (maybe North Kannapolis), still has some goodies to tell about life there a long time ago, like the 1920s.

First the judge: "The Old Lutheran Cemetery on East Corban Street in Concord is a place of memories," he wrote. "In simpler times, it was a place where families gathered to mourn and to remember, to place or plant flowers, to carefully tend the graves of loved ones.

"Now it is a place of fallen and crumbling tombstones and ill-tended plots, a monument to the brevity of human memory."

There'll be more below—but now, our old-timey Unknown Writer has more fun to share.

> *Back in the early '20s, up in North Kannapolis, there was a Houser Oil Co. had one gas pump that had a handle that was pushed back and forward pumping the gas up into the glass container on top until you got how much gas you wanted, then run it in car through a hose, like today.*
>
> *Houser also sold Model-T Fords.*
>
> *One Saturday, Granddaddy W.D. got up and, as usual, got ready to go to Kannapolis. But unbeknown to anyone, he went to Houser's and bought a new Model T Ford.*
>
> *They showed him all about how to start and drive it. First time ever behind a steering wheel.*
>
> *Off he went up to the railroad crossing. Missed the road but bounced across the tracks.*

But the folks at Houser's hadn't shown him how to stop.

> *Around his house a few times and got it headed toward my Granddaddy's house.*
>
> *They all rushed out to see what was going on. Going around in circles in the barnyard, hollering, "It won't stop!"*
>
> *Got the Model T headed back to his house, and more times around the house.*

Had left horse and buggy in North Kannapolis, so the buggy shed was empty. Maybe if he could put it there it would stop.

The brand new Model T knocked the back out of the buggy shed and kept going.

After getting it stopped, W.D. never drove it again. But anytime he wanted to go in the Model T Ford, my daddy's 13-year-old brother was ready to take him.

People, it's hard to find much better readin' than some of the anecdotes old-timers come up with, like the letters from our still anonymous writer.

Now back to the cemetery. Judge Horton has provided us with many articulate, thought-provoking articles, and in his essay on that fading Lutheran cemetery, he quotes local lawyer Jim Johnson, a well-known collector of all things military who has warehouses crammed with his amazing collections from all wars.

Johnson, the judge wrote, deems it "a tragedy that those who protected our borders and shaped our beginnings do not enjoy the respect of a well-kept resting place.

"Revolutionary War soldiers, two militia Generals, the Captain of Cabarrus County Volunteers in the Mexican War, and a host of men who honorably served in the Civil War are all buried in the cemetery.

"It is a shame that we cannot even locate some of their graves now."

11.

Quaint Epitaph—and Thousands Flock
to Big July Fourth Parade

Sunday, June 7, 1992

It's quaint and sad, this two-hundred-year-old epitaph at historic old Coddle Creek ARP Church:

Here
Lys Ye Bod
of James
Caruth who
Deceased Decemb[er]
Ye 9th *1757 Aged 27*
years also he[re]
Lys His son Alexand[er]
Caruth who Decea[sed]
Nov. Ye 22, 1778 age
22 years

One only had to say the word "parade" and Kannapolis folks went all out. The striking Patriotic Order Sons of America float above made its way over the main street in a 1920s July Fourth event.

Yes, folks, there really are possums in that tree on a float in a 1949 Christmas parade in the Towel City.

James Caruth was a member of historic Coddle Creek Associate Reformed Presbyterian Church, which is still on North Carolina 136 just across the Cabarrus County line in Iredell County.

Caruth and his wife, Sarah, came here from Pennsylvania and settled by Coddle Creek, near Rocky River. His tombstone is the oldest still legible in that old cemetery. His son died even younger than he did. Historians date Coddle Creek Church to 1753, and claim it's the oldest of the four to five hundred churches in the entire General Synod of the Associate Reformed Presbyterian Church.

In the same issue of the late L.D. Coltrane Jr.'s *Progress* magazine, there's also a story of a rousing old-timey Fourth of July in Kannapolis.

Viewers roared with laughter at the man on a mule, waving his political poster in a 1952 parade put on by Kannapolis Jaycees (Junior Chamber of Commerce).

Even in the grim Depression years of the 1930s, when July Fourth rolled around, Kannapolis folks went all out to put on a rousing patriotic parade. "The parade formed around the lake," the article begins, "then flags waved, bands played and the very heavens rang with the shouts of the throng when the bands played 'Dixie!'

"There were drum and bugle corps bands, National Guard units, Spanish-American and World War I veterans and a bevy of beautiful girls." A center of attention was "several cars filled with the few remaining veterans of the Civil War."

Mind you, these July Fourth parades were all-day celebrations. "And thrilling they were," says the *Progress* article. "The pomp, ceremony, bands, floats, baseball games and large crowds contributed to a great and glorious celebration.

"A brilliant display of fireworks over the lake was the climax of a day long to be remembered. This event was the result of many months of planning and hard work by a lot of people."

In the '30s I remember vividly seeing the high-stepping drum major, the late Brice "Bub" Willeford Sr., wearing a sparkling white uniform and white shako hat. He led the band, leaning into deep, graceful backbends as he strutted back and forth. And, ah, those floats! The article continued, "Although there may be some question as to the artistic appearance, it's obvious they were original. Remember, suitable material was hard to find" because money was scarce in those days.

The parade was so big people came from far away "to spend the day with friends and kin, to see the parade, to eat a big dinner and just to visit." Main Street was "lined with men, women and children ten or twelve deep, from the square to C Street." Kannapolis planned a giant old-fashioned Fourth of July celebration again in 1992 to celebrate Cabarrus County's bicentennial year.

12.

Kannapolis's Earliest Settler:
Prominent John Baker Sr.

Sunday, November 11, 1990

Kannapolis may be the new town in Cabarrus County, emerging as a budding Cannon Mills village around 1906, growing mightily and, just six years ago, incorporating as a city. But its gently rolling, sprawling lands, so busily urban today, have a history as ancient as any hereabouts.

Buffalo and a multitude of other early animals roamed there. Some of our earliest pioneers—one enterprising John Baker Sr. among them—penetrated its forests and fields to raise their primitive homesteads and families, to worship, to farm and to spend the rest of their lives. And Kannapolis soil still holds the bones of some of our early ancestors.

Just last Sunday, area historians and heritage buffs dedicated a historical marker in honor of John Baker Sr., who pioneered this area in the 1770s and is believed to be Kannapolis's earliest settler. A lot of modern Kannapolis folks—many of them Baker's descendants—flocked to the old cemetery dedication to do him honor.

The Baker monument is the oldest marked grave in the Kannapolis Cemetery. Mr. Baker owned much land in the late 1700s where Kannapolis now stands.

For John Baker Sr. flourished here, an influential man and a man of property, including much that today is downtown Kannapolis. He had many children and descendants. Even his marker, a handsome, graying, star-dotted soapstone tombstone, bears the delightfully grim old epitaph:

Remember man, as you pass by,
As you are now, so once was I.
As I am now, so must you be,
Prepare for Death to follow me.

Today, Baker's tombstone, under two oak trees near the cemetery wall, is the oldest identifiable marker in Kannapolis Cemetery. His wife, Sarah, has a similar soapstone tombstone nearby.

John Baker was known as a gentleman pioneer. His story is engaging, and for the information, thanks go to several prominent Towel Citizens, including historians Tom Wingate, J.K. Rouse and Judge Clarence Horton, among others.

Around 1772 or 1773, Baker came to this area—then part of Mecklenburg County—and acquired property from one John Lewis Beard, who himself had acquired it through a grant from King George III of England in 1761, area historians say.

No one knows why John Baker came to this then-backwoods wilderness. Some historians believe he came to be near his brothers Christopher, Joshua, Benjamin, Absalom Jr., Samuel and Greenberry; his sister, Margaret Baker; and his father, Absalom Baker. They mostly lived in Rowan County, not far from John, who settled near Buffalo Creek. Over the years John Baker used his knack for making profitable trades and deals and amassed a fortune in the process. He kept a sharp eye out for good land and when he spotted some, he'd secure a grant from the state of North Carolina, hold the property for a few years and sell it at a satisfying profit to new settlers.

Baker also wielded some influence and had influential friends and neighbors in early Cabarrus, especially the legendary Phifers, the Revolutionary War heroes who also served in the Colonial Assembly and entertained the likes of President George Washington and Royal Governor William Tryon.

John Baker's death in 1816, however, was sudden and of an unknown illness. He left no will, so the Cabarrus Court of Pleas and Quarter Sessions was responsible for dividing his estate. It included 958 acres in Rowan and Cabarrus Counties, twelve slaves, real property and quantities of livestock that were divided among his children, John Jr., Richmond, Joseph, Joshua, Benjamin, Mary, Eleanor and Griffeth.

Son Joseph lived all his life in the Kannapolis area, and his descendants still live here in great numbers, among them Winecoffs, Goodnights, Harts, Pennys, Seafords and Overcashes. Joseph's early life, filled with hard labor, historians say, became easier after he inherited slaves from his father's estate. Joseph also was a faithful member and elder of Bethpage Presbyterian Church. In 1840 he gave twenty-five dollars cash, fourteen pieces of lumber and four thousand shingles to help build it. He's buried in the church cemetery.

Today, if the old pioneer John Baker could emerge from his grave under those two oak trees near the cemetery entrance, he would be amazed to see what happened to his eighteenth-century farm, wrote Tom Wingate, retired editor of the *Daily Independent*.

He might be even more shocked, historian Wingate wrote, on seeing his great-great-great-grandchildren gathered around his grave two centuries later, paying him homage in a touching ritual. It might surprise him and maybe rile him a bit to learn that his family cemetery, long called Baker Cemetery, had grown and acquired a new name, Kannapolis Cemetery.

Baker's Cemetery on His 1700s Royal Land Grant

Sunday, November 18, 1990

On the brand-new marker in Kannapolis Cemetery—ten years in the making, dedicated November 4 to honor Baker—is a simple message:

Historic Kannapolis Cemetery.
Originally known as Baker Cemetery.
Site of the graves of John Baker Sr., Born October 12, 1745,
Died January 18, 1816, his family and descendants.
Many early settlers, veterans and citizens of Kannapolis
are buried here.

Pioneer Baker may have made history, of a sort, Tom Wingate believes.

Around 1772, as America's Revolutionary War was beginning to boil, Baker got a land grant of one hundred acres from King George III of England. Baker's grant, Wingate has written, may have been one of the last official acts of English colonial government in North Carolina before the Revolution began. The grant was issued to Baker by Josiah Martin, North Carolina's last royal governor. In these and other writings on the old pioneer, I haven't yet found, from whence John Baker or his father, Absalom, hailed.

John Baker, however, did make his trek to this wilderness area in the 1770s and settled down to pioneering with his wife, Sarah, for the rest of his seventy-one years and four months of life.

Today, most of those historic Baker properties are covered over by the Cannon Memorial Library, the David Murdock Senior Center, the Cannon Memorial YMCA, Kannapolis Cemetery "and most of the residential and business property on both sides of Buffalo Creek and both sides of the county line," Wingate wrote.

In 1792—the same year that Cabarrus County folk won the battle to create their new county out of Mecklenburg—Baker bought two hundred more acres from one Christopher Holler for eleven English pounds "in current money," according to Wingate. These acres today are home to the sprawling Fieldcrest Cannon complex, a portion of downtown Kannapolis and the dense residential districts in west Kannapolis.

So it would seem that nearly anywhere citizens go in or around Kannapolis, they will cross, at many points, acreage that was once old

John Baker's. After John Baker died, his daughter Mary inherited the land that today is Kannapolis Cemetery.

Historian Wingate found that Mary and her husband, Charles Baker (records don't indicate whether they were related by blood), sold her inheritance in order to go to Franklin County, Georgia, where some Indian lands had been confiscated and were put up in a lottery. Mary's inheritance was sold for $500 (about $2.50 an acre) to Robert Ramsey of Franklin County, Georgia, as shown by a deed dated April 17, 1820. Ramsey then turned around ten days later and sold Mary's inheritance to John Rogers of Cabarrus and Rowan Counties—for $500. The cemetery property eventually came full circle, returning to Baker ownership in 1824 when Rogers sold it to Mary's brother Joseph for $475.

"It is believed," wrote historian Wingate, "that the 61¼-acre share of Baker family lands that [eventually] went to Martha B. [Mrs. J. Wallace] Cook included the family burying ground.

"That acreage was purchased in 1906 by the late James W. Cannon [founder of Cannon Mills] and became a prominent part of what is now the proud city of Kannapolis."

13.

Varied and Colorful History in Old Coleman Community

Monday, May 20, 2002, and Sunday, June 30, 2002

The Coleman community, which straddled the Cabarrus-Rowan County Line near Kannapolis for a couple of hundred years, was never a town, just a loose conglomeration of small farms.

In its heyday, Coleman had at most a post office, a Masonic lodge, maybe a general store and a cotton gin—and lots of Kannapolis and southern Rowan County names, according to an article written by late Kannapolis historian J.K. Rouse. But Coleman's local history probably goes back to 1770 and before. Rouse's history sort of bounces up and down through the Coleman area and through the ages, and thanks to Guy Beaver Jr., I have a copy of that article.

Historian Rouse's work touches on President George Washington, Crystal Springs Presbyterian Church, the death of an 1800s state politician, the Great Wagon Road, Cannon Mills founder J.W. Cannon and the death of a young doctor—to mention a few of the topics.

It opens with a land sale in 1822, when Jacob B. Coleman bought 233 acres from Joshua Baker, son of wealthy Kannapolis pioneer John Baker.

The property lay on the Great Wagon Road, an ancient Indian trail that cut through Kannapolis in upper Cabarrus County that later sent hordes of European pioneers into this area. The newly acquired Coleman property, on Reedy Creek, adjoined the lands of Revolutionary War hero Martin Phifer. The creek runs southward, passing behind Kannapolis's A.L. Brown High School, Rouse wrote.

Rouse brings in old Crystal Springs Church, a little Presbyterian church in southern Rowan County. Joseph McPherson, Robert McPherson, John Driskel and property buyer John Long all were listed as original members, he wrote, and in 1770 they all petitioned the presbytery in New York to supply them with a minister and church needs.

A History of Rowan County by Dr. Jethro Rumple claims that Crystal Springs Church "had difficulty in securing a minister" and therefore closed its doors in 1804. As a result, many of Crystal Springs Church's members transferred to the old Bethpage Presbyterian Church near Enochville, west of what is now Kannapolis.

An interesting sidelight, Rouse wrote, is that in 1836, Bethpage Church made a list of members of the congregation who made a donation to Davidson College and Jacob Coleman was on that list. Jacob Coleman had bought the Great Wagon Road property because of its location on "a much traveled road" in the Piedmont. President Washington had ridden over it on his famed Southern tour to visit Charlotte.

Now for the father of our country. Rouse quoted records that showed that on Sunday, May 29, 1791, President Washington ate a "sumptuous" meal at the Colonel Robert Smith home (which stood on the current Lowe's Motor Speedway site). Afterward the president rode to the tavern and home of Colonel Martin Phifer, who had fought under Washington during the Revolution. Washington "slept here" with the Phifers in Cabarrus County.

The next day, Washington and his entourage traveled northward through what is now Kannapolis into Rowan County, where they were met at the county line by Captain John Beard "and his company of Light Dragoons," who took the presidential entourage to Captain Edward Yarborough's Rowan County tavern for breakfast.

Now Rouse's account takes on another twist and turn. On May 24, 1822, a southbound stagecoach stopped at the tavern of George Savitz, near China Grove. Out of the coach stepped U.S. Representative James Overstreet, who represented the Barnwell district in South Carolina.

Overstreet had just completed his second term in Congress and was homeward bound with his wife, Agnes Mary. But almost immediately after arriving at the tavern, the congressman suffered a heart attack and died.

"We know that funeral rites were conducted by the Masonic Lodge of Salisbury," Rouse wrote, "and that he was buried in the Savitz graveyard at Mount Zion Reformed Church of China Grove."

Later, Agnes Mary erected a tall white monument at his grave. It read: "Sacred to the memory of James Overstreet, who was a member from South Carolina in the 17th Congress and died on his way from Washington City to his residence the 24th day of May 1822, age 49 years, 3 months and 13 days.

"He was an affectionate husband, a good father and undeviating Republican. No further seek his merits to disclose or draw his frailties from their dread abode; there they alike in trembling hope repose the bosom of his Father and his God."

Fast forward to 1836, when the Coleman community needed better mail service, Rouse wrote, so Jacob B. Coleman was appointed postmaster. But that was after a political friend from Concord had been appointed by President Andrew Jackson as assistant postmaster general of the United States. "Having a friend in Washington as Assistant Postmaster General perhaps made it easy for Jacob Coleman to receive the appointment as postmaster," Rouse wrote.

Before long, the Coleman community attracted a young doctor to practice among them. Before the Civil War, rural communities in Cabarrus County were seldom able to get such services, Rouse wrote. Dr. Franklin Chaffin had studied under a celebrated schoolmaster,

Peter Stewart Ney, "who many believe today to have been the great Marshal Ney, a soldier under Napoleon Bonaparte of France," Rouse wrote.

In 1850, the seventh census of Cabarrus County lists Jacob B. Coleman, sixty-seven, a farmer and Cabarrus native, living with his sixty-four-year-old wife, Mary; a thirteen-year-old girl named Josephine DeMarcus; and a twenty-one-year-old laborer, Fielding Montgomery. Jacob seems to have prospered: He owned 537 acres, valued at $2,610, and four slaves. He lived a long time for back then, dying at age eighty-one.

Perhaps the most significant event in the first hundred years of the Coleman community, Rouse concluded, was the purchase of many of its small farms by James William Cannon of Concord. That land, of course, ultimately went on to house an impressive international textile empire: Cannon Mills Company, maker of quality towels, sheets, pillowcases and other accessories.

It's easy to see why the Coleman community was so named but sad to see that its existence is all but forgotten, except for J.K. Rouse and his colorful recording of its history.

14.

Kannapolis's Israel Pickens Made Vital Alabama History

Sunday, July 5, 1992

When Alabama's history is told, it could almost begin with a Kannapolis area native who piled up political successes and even some scientific coups after he left Cabarrus County in the late 1700s. Meet Israel Pickens, born west of Kannapolis (now Township 3) on January 30, 1780, who became the third governor of Alabama—and the first Alabama governor to serve a full term. During Pickens's impressive career, he was elected to the North Carolina legislature and the U.S. Congress. He was also appointed U.S. senator and served as a member of Alabama's 1819 Constitutional Convention.

While still a teenager fascinated by science and mathematics, he invented a lunar dial by which the time of night could be determined by the moon. One of Pickens's early tutors was "the Rev. Doctor Hale, a celebrated mathematician of that period,"

Marie Owens wrote in *The Story of Alabama*. "Israel possessed extraordinary mechanical ingenuity and showed a great fondness for mathematics, natural philosophy and astronomy," he added.

Cabarrus County, of course, was still Mecklenburg County in 1780, when Israel Pickens was born to former Revolutionary soldier Captain Samuel Pickens and Jane Carrigan Pickens. The site of his birth in present-day Cabarrus County is still unknown. Young Israel was named for his grandfather, Israel Pickens, a descendant of a French Huguenot family who came to America about 1722, settled in Bucks County, Pennsylvania, then later moved to Cabarrus County. Unfortunately, the date they arrived in the county is unknown, according to information from retired Kannapolis editor Tom Wingate.

Young Israel had an outstanding education, claim several Alabama history sources, as well as the bicentennial edition of the *Biographical Directory of the United States Congress*, published in 1988. He studied under private teachers, at schools in Iredell County, attended Jefferson College and graduated from Washington College, both in Pennsylvania in 1802. Young Israel soon was admitted to the North Carolina State Bar.

Early on, young Israel's multiple abilities became apparent, and his continuing career in politics was off and running. He served in North Carolina's "Upper House" in 1808–09 and in the U.S. House of Representatives 1811–17.

So far no historian has written why, after all his success, Israel Pickens moved—with his wife, Martha Orilla—to Alabama in 1817.

In June 1814, he was married to Martha Orilla Lenoir, daughter of General William Lenoir. In February 1826, he was appointed to fill a vacancy in the U.S. Senate, but he decided not to run for a full term in the office in November 1826. When Israel and Martha Orilla moved to St. Stephens in 1817, Alabama was still a part of the Mississippi Territory—a wilderness still inhabited by American Indians. That then-territory was known as "Tombeckbee Country" and "was attracting the attention of ambitious young men from the older states," Owens wrote.

Pickens represented Washington County in the state's constitutional convention at Huntsville in 1819. "Owing to the untimely death of William Wyatt Bibb, the first governor of the state, and the temporary service of his brother, Thomas Bibb, as acting governor, the task of actually organizing and establishing state government in Alabama on a firm foundation fell to Israel Pickens. There, Pickens was a register in the land office of that territory."

He was first elected Alabama governor in 1821.

Of the Kannapolis native, J.C. Stewart wrote in *The Governors of Alabama*:

> *With Israel Pickens, native North Carolinian…may be dated the beginning of definite political alliances and vigorous political battles in Alabama…*[He] *was the first to serve a full term as governor.*
>
> *He* [Pickens] *served two terms, in fact, and turned the political tide against the Georgia machine, which had supported his two predecessors and had come to represent, in the eyes of the average voter, the interests of the aristocratic, the monied, and the powerful.*
>
> *Paradoxically, Pickens himself was a man of aristocratic background, well educated, and not entirely outside the circle of monied interests…*
>
> *But following the depression of 1819,* [Pickens] *apparently saw the need for a state bank, as a government-controlled assist to the people who had lost money and had little credit left.*
>
> *Again, paradoxically, although he and Andrew Jackson seemed in perfect accord concerning the interests of the common man, they differed on the banking question.*
>
> *Jackson opposed the state-owned bank.*

But when Pickens ran for his second term as Alabama governor, in 1823, banking was the prime—indeed the only—issue, Stewart wrote.

And when Pickens for the second time defeated his opponent, Dr. Henry Chambers of Madison County, Georgia—the candidate of the Georgia machine—politics began to bubble.

"Even at the early stage in Alabama history, the old division of interests between the haves and have-nots asserted itself...

"The spokesman for the have-nots was Israel Pickens."

Pickens, indeed, was in high 1800s cotton with the likes of Andrew Jackson and with Georgia's Chambers and Crawford of that once powerful political machine.

In 1992, North Carolina acknowledged the accomplishments of this native Tarheel by erecting a highway historical marker in his honor.

Israel Pickens "is considered the outstanding governor prior to the Civil War," claims his biographer in *The Governors of Alabama*.

Even so, Israel Pickens showed some very human characteristics.

During Pickens's second term as governor of Alabama, 1823–26, the Marquis de Lafayette, that great Frenchman whose efforts helped America win the American Revolution, passed through Alabama on his way to New Orleans, the biographer wrote.

"A grand reception was planned for [Lafayette] in Alabama, where he would be formally welcomed to the state," he continued. As governor, Israel Pickens was to conduct the formal proceedings. As hero Lafayette traveled from Georgia into Alabama, and was met at Fort Mitchell by a welcoming party, including Pickens, who had come there by boat. "After a day of wild demonstrations of joy," wrote Marie Owens, "the governor escorted Lafayette to the capital city of Cahaba, where he was welcomed by an address and dinner, after which the general departed by river for Mobile."

However, another biographer wrote, "Pickens was so overawed by the popular French hero that he was unable to speak, and Bolling Hall had to deliver the formal greeting."

"His experience in state politics in North Carolina, three terms in Congress and his constant contacts with the citizens of Alabama while registrar of the land office gave him a familiarity with the problems of the state that no other man possessed," wrote the biographer.

"Cahaba had previously been designated as the state capital, and though lots had been sold and homes had begun to be built, it became Governor Pickens' duty to complete the construction of the Capitol building and actually develop a capital city."

In new Alabama, Pickens also helped create judicial circuits, new counties and new roads.

"The governor had almost complete control of the legislature," Owens wrote, "even though he had broken with the political clique that had supported William Wyatt Bibb.

"At this time there were no well-defined party lines in Alabama, but the northern and southern halves of the state generally opposed each other on most candidates and political issues.

"Pickens created a political machine of his own, but it was destined to break up over the issues of the State Bank and the election of Governor Joshua Martin as an independent candidate in 1845"—eighteen years after Pickens's death.

Handsome and Accomplished, Pickens Seemed Paragon of Virtue

Sunday, July 19, 1992

Israel Pickens seems to have been a paragon of virtue. And with good looks, accomplishments and integrity, according to new biographical information I received. "Governor Pickens was six feet high…very slender and erect," reads a short biography compiled in 1935 by the late Mary Lore Flowe of Concord, a descendant. His complexion was fair and his eyes were blue.

"In all attributes of moral nature he was indeed a remarkable man. His manners were easy, affable and kind—his temper mild, amiable and always the same. Benevolence was a predominant trait in his character. He had a finished education and talents of a high order and more solid than brilliant. As a public man, he was very popular and although mild and gentle in his deportment, no one was firmer in the discharge of his public duties. He possessed extraordinary mechanical ingenuity and a great fondness for mathematics, natural philosophy and astronomy."

That mathematical know-how once enabled Israel Pickens to expose a man in Washington who pretended to have discovered the secrets of perpetual motion.

The man—his last name was Reidheifer, Flowe wrote—had built a "perpetual motion" machine, which he exhibited to members of Congress, Israel Pickens among them.

"Being satisfied there was deception...[Pickens] returned the next day and gave it a more thorough examination," as the door was unlocked and no one was present in the room. "During this second visit [Pickens] detected the fraud and exposed it, by inserting a card in the National Intelligencer, signed 'A Member of Congress.'

"This brought forth a bitter reply from the impostor...but in a few days, Reidheifer, model and all left the city, never to return."

The Flowe account tells us that "while living in Morganton, the romance of [Israel Pickens's] life came into being.

"Not far away lived the lovely Martha Orilla LeNoir, daughter of Gen. William and Ann Ballard LeNoir, and their marriage took place [June 9, 1814] in the ancestral home which is still in possession of the family...

"Four children were born to this union, three growing to mature years, Julia Ann Mira, Andrew LeNoir, Israel Leonidas and William James.

"Among the treasures at the old LeNoir home in Wilkes County are dresses worn by Patsy [Martha's nickname] while she was with her husband in Washington, letters to her brother when she was attending school in Raleigh and Salem, the letter from Israel Pickens to Gen. LeNoir asking permission to pursue his suit, and letters from Washington telling of affairs there."

The Flowe account and others add a bit as to Israel's birthplace and early life. Israel Pickens's ancestors came to America from Limerick, Ireland, in 1697. In 1743, after the Pickenses arrived in Cabarrus County, they occupied a homestead west of Kannapolis, "now owned [in 1935] by Dr. E.R. Harris." It seems Israel Pickens was born in 1780 in an area west of Kannapolis.

Young Israel was "brought up and educated in this neighborhood under the tutelage of Dr. Archibald Robinson, then the accomplished preceptor of an Academy at Poplar Tent."

It wouldn't surprise me if, after reading about this distinguished Pickens, many Cabarrus folk began rummaging through their genealogy to find a family connection. I've learned that old Andrew Pickens arrived in north Cabarrus County with an 808-acre grant, and soon became well known as a landed proprietor, a captain in the North Carolina militia, a majesty's justice and a substantial family man.

His descendant, Israel, had three surviving children—Julia, Andrew and Israel—and four brothers and two sisters. Their descendants today include Flowes, Barnhardts, Walkups and Howes, among many other area surnames.

While a U.S. senator, Israel Pickens urged war with England, whose harassment of U.S. merchant vessels led to the War of 1812. He advocated taxing salt, liquor stills and slaves to pay for the war. Pickens was also president of the Alabama Colonization Society, whose goal was to free the slaves and return them, as free men, to a colony in Africa.

While living in Washington, the couple had moved in sophisticated circles, enjoyed an elegant lifestyle and mingled with presidents and first ladies and leading political figures.

Dolley Madison was a particular friend of Patsy, who received her education in Raleigh.

It must have been a happy time on January 6, 1818, when Israel and his beloved wife, Martha arrived in Alabama, then mainly inhabited by Indians.

In his letter home describing their trip, Israel wrote, "My family and I at length reached our destination...without any accidents or misfortune...making our journey near six weeks.

Indians were very civil and we had no apprehension of them, though we traveled without any other than our own company... The road was bad beyond conception for about eighty miles, almost continuous swamp. We passed many wagons and other carriages...some broken and some stuck in the mud.

"The little galley [carriage] has carried us safe through every swamp. Our horses performed admirably.

"Every house here, public and private, is filled—such is the crowd of strangers and immigrants.

"We had shelter in our own little log house, which I had raised last summer when I came out to examine the land. By scuffling about, we have already made it quite comfortable...[and] are as comfortably situated as any of the gentry, though not so stylish."

In 1821 they left their log cabin for Greenwood, the plantation Israel built three miles from Greensboro, Alabama. So Greenwood became, Owens wrote, "a beautiful, two-story residence...seated upon an elevation that spread out into hundreds of acres... cultivated in a scientific manner by slaves under the intelligent direction of a master whom history has recorded as one of the great State builders."

Patsy Pickens, as Alabama's first lady, planted flowers and brought in fine mahogany furniture, china, crystal and linens.

Their lovely time at Greenwood, however, was short-lived. At thirty-one, Patsy Pickens died of malaria. She had just returned to Greenwood from a spring visit with her parents in North Carolina. That fall Patsy and Israel's baby son, James, also died.

Israel died April 24, 1827, at age forty-seven, and was buried in Cuba, where he had gone for treatment of tuberculosis. Years later, caring relatives brought Israel's remains to Greenwood and buried them beside his beloved Patsy in the private burial grounds on the plantation.

Flowe claims, "From [Israel Pickens's] dead body, the silhouette portrait of Patsy, his beloved wife was found by his brother and brought back, and his letter to his father-in-law telling of her death paid a beautiful tribute to her." Several years after

Pickens's death, the Greenwood plantation house was moved to Greensboro, Alabama, and in 1933, the bodies of the Pickens family were moved to a cemetery in Greensboro.

The loss of Israel Pickens was a severe one, wrote Willis Brewer in his history of Alabama. "For he possessed the solid, ingenious and practical talents [a new state] needs; the experience to shape her domestic polity; and the wisdom and virtue…all governments should leave as a legacy to posterity."

Towel City in Pictures

S ince the historic face of Kannapolis has so abruptly disappeared through the razing of those staunch old Cannon Mills plants, it seems appropriate to include some vintage photographs of the life and times of old Kannapolis.

For not only the physical face will change, but the entire culture— the Kannapolis way of life—will undergo a radical transformation when billionaire David Murdock's ambitious food and nutrition research center is complete. Thousands of high-tech researchers and workers are expected to flood this old cotton mill town and give it an awesome new look.

So we feel it important, even necessary, to preserve some special reminders of what Kannapolis was—its special old ways, its successes and its heritage.

Today Towel Citizens can thank Larry Hayer, local history librarian, and his volunteers in the Kannapolis branch library, for gathering, sorting and filing these choice images safely away in history room records.

So enjoy this photographic stroll down memory lane.

The ancient Chambers house was known as a bootlegger's lair, built back before Kannapolis was born. Most likely, moonshine was made and sold there. Unfortunately, the house disappeared years ago. The people posing for the photographer are not identified.

Kannapolis people loved racing and racers, especially the late Ralph Earnhardt, Kannapolis native and father of the winning driver, the late Dale Earnhardt. Ralph, beside the 1952 race cars, chats with men identified only as M. Burris and B. Connell.

Early on, Towel Citizens exhibited a love of music, and in 1921 built a bandstand in the town lake, where the mill band performed. The man pictured is Harvey Turner Sr., whose son Harvey Jr. later was director of Kannapolis's Brown High Band.

This rare 1900 photograph shows a group of young children who were working at Gibson Mill in nearby Concord for long hours every day. This was the case in many towns over the United States in those early years. The children are not identified.

In 1945, Charles Cannon had many of these four-hundred-square-foot houses built for returning war veterans and their families. They called the area GI Town. Though small, families loved them. One is now a World War II memorial house and museum with a Chrysler Jeep command car out front.

Back in 1932, Cannon Mills had its own band, which gave concerts on occasion, wearing their white uniforms. Above, they're playing in front of the YMCA. In later years, the band dissolved.

Patriotic to the core, a group of World War I Kannapolis vets got a wooden replica of a World War II tank and were using it to help sell war bonds, beside the town lake.

For many years, a large white billboard stood by the lakeside park downtown, bearing the names of all area World War II veterans. They called it Little Mount Vernon or the Little White House. Unfortunately, it proved too expensive to keep up and was ultimately destroyed.

The YMCA, next to the mills, was the lifeblood of Kannapolis from day one. In time, it offered any service any activity, Towel Citizens could have ever wanted. In its heyday, there were thirty thousand members who paid a joining fee of one dollar. There were three Y buildings, the third shown in the photo. It was destroyed in 1987.

In the 1940s, Kannapolis's love of baseball crystallized in an unusually successful American Legion team. Players traveled to far-off games in a giant plane, shown in this photo.

A sad day. Kannapolis people cried as a major old Cannon plant was razed, showing only a water tower and the distribution center above the rubble. There's hope, though, as billionaire David Murdock is building a billion-dollar new research center downtown.

Charles Cannon, president of Cannon Mills, is presented with his fifty-year pin by another fifty-year employee, Oscar Towell, known as Oss. Charles Cannon held his Loyalty Banquets every year to honor his loyal mill employees of five or more years.

For years, President Cannon promised his workers, "We'll put our feet under the same table as long as we can," with Loyalty Banquets at the YMCA. When there were too many employees to find a place to serve them, they were replaced with big outdoor picnics.

Kannapolis's volunteer firemen race with fire hoses in a 1927 competition. They performed well against teams from surrounding towns. They were judged on speed getting to fire scenes, running with hoses, pumping water from hauled vats—a far cry from modern techniques.

NASCAR's winningest driver, the late Dale Earnhardt, celebrates a big win at the Darlington, South Carolina racetrack in 1986. Earnhardt, a Kannapolis native, is probably the most adored man in his hometown. Local folk, mourning his death, erected a king-sized statue of their idol and centered it in a park downtown, in his honor and to his memory. *Photo courtesy of the* Charlotte Observer.

Dale Earnhardt is photographed during a pensive moment in 1991, wearing his racing coverall. After his death, countless racing fans across the United States mourned with Kannapolis folk. *Photo courtesy of the Charlotte Observer.*

Dale Earnhardt, who won many NASCAR racing events and championships, is shown autographing a picture for fan Allan Waddell at the old Charlotte Motor Speedway (now Lowe's Motor Speedway) in Charlotte. An aggressive racer, he was nicknamed the Intimidator. *Photo courtesy of the* Charlotte Observer.

Charles Cannon.

1968 postcard of Cannon Mills.

This 2005 photo was taken just before Plant One was demolished, making way for a new biotech research center.

Please visit us at
www.historypress.net